Hedge Funds and Prime Brokers

Hedge Funds and Prime Brokers

Edited by Mark Berman

Published by Risk Books, a Division of Incisive Financial Publishing Ltd

Haymarket House
28–29 Haymarket
London SW1Y 4RX
Tel: +44 (0)20 7484 9700
Fax: +44 (0)20 7484 9800
E-mail: books@incisivemedia.com
Sites: www.riskbooks.com
         www.incisivemedia.com

ISBN 1 904 399 905

British Library Cataloguing in Publication Data
A catalogue record for this book is available from the British Library

Publisher: Laurie Donaldson
Assistant Editor: Steve Fairman
Designer: Rebecca Bramwell

Typeset by Mizpah Publishing Services Private Limited, Chennai, India

Printed and bound in Spain by Espacegrafic, Pamplona, Navarra

Conditions of sale

Contents

About the Authors

Deborah Anthony is a tax partner with Deloitte's Financial Service Practice in London. She leads the UK hedge fund tax practice as well as working in the private equity area. Debbie has spent many years working in the financial services sector for clients ranging from international financial institutions to the private equity/ hedge fund sector, where she advises a number of leading funds. She is a regular speaker at conferences in this area.

Diya Agarwal is an experienced Deloitte's corporate tax senior manager specialising in the hedge fund services practice, and is responsible for servicing inbound hedge fund start-ups together with well-established UK managers. Diya joined Andersen London in 1999 and subsequently joined Deloitte London after the transaction in 2002.Diya received a degree in mathematics from Bristol University. She joined Andersen as a scholar in 1995 and a graduate in 1999. She became a fully qualified member of the Institute of Chartered Accountants in England and Wales in 2002.

Barry P. Barbash is a partner with the law firm of Willkie Farr & Gallagher LLP. He is the head of the firm's Asset Management Group and member of the firm's Executive Committee. He is a former director of the US Securities and Exchange Commission's Division of Investment Management, serving in that capacity from September 1993 until October 1998. Barry has a diverse practice covering all aspects of the asset management business. He regularly advises mutual fund and hedge fund clients on a variety of transactional, compliance and regulatory matters. He was ranked in the number 1 tier for leading individuals practicing investment management law in Washington, D.C. by *Chambers USA* (2006). Barry is a 1978 graduate of Cornell Law School with a J.D. degree and a 1975 graduate of Bowdoin College with an A.B. degree, summa cum laude. He is a member of the New York, District of Columbia and Massachusetts Bars.

Larry E. Bergmann is special counsel to Willkie Farr & Gallagher LLP in Washington DC. Larry concentrates on complex SEC regulatory matters and securities law matters, with a focus on trading and underwriting issues, broker–dealer compliance, securities analysis, issuer repurchases, transfer agents and enforcement-related matters. He served with the US Securities and Exchange Commission for 31 years, in the Northeast Regional Office, in the Division of Enforcement and in the Division of Market Regulation where, latterly, he served as senior associate director. His responsibilities included administering the SEC's trading practices rules, rules applying to short sales and research analysts and "soft dollar" interpretations. He supervised the Commission's oversight program for clearing agencies and transfer agents, and the Division of Market Regulation's Enforcement Liaison Office. He received numerous awards, including the Commission's Distinguished Service Award, and the Presidential Rank Meritorious Service Award. Larry is a member of the American Bar Association.

Mark Berman advises and has advised investment managers, hedge funds (including the Threadneedle Crescendo hedge funds), multi-national banks, investment firms and ATSs on cross-border legal, compliance, regulatory and AML matters. He is the editor of and a contributor to *SEC Regulation Outside the United States* (5th ed. 2005, Risk Books), and founded and chairs a conference by same name, held annually in London and in Hong Kong. Mr Berman was a senior lawyer with the SEC's Division of Corporation Finance and the Division of Market Regulation, where he worked on domestic and international disclosure and trading practices issues. He was a senior lawyer with the London Stock Exchange. Mark has lectured on law and finance at the London Business School, and is a Trustee of the SEC Historical Society.

Patrick Connolly is a technical audit manager in the Financial Services Industry group at Deloitte Dublin. He has over eight years experience of auditing offshore funds located in Dublin. He has written topical articles on funds for Dublin-based industry publications and lectured on financial reporting practices to the Irish Fund's Industry Association's Diploma in Mutual Fund Services class for 2005/2006. He is a first class honours commerce graduate of University College Dublin and has a first class Master of Accounting degree (UCD, 1995). He is a member of the Institute of Chartered Accountants of Ireland.

Paul Dentskevich is a portfolio manager at HSH Nordbank AG, where he is co-responsible for the banks proprietary investment in hedge funds (internal fund of hedge funds). He has a diverse finance background and has worked on both the buy- and the sell-side. During his career, Paul has been a hedge fund risk manager and has developed and implemented advanced risk methodologies and systems and complex derivative structures. He has published papers on risk methodologies and derivative pricing and chaired and presented at numerous international risk-based conferences. Paul holds a PhD in economics and finance, an MSc in management science and a BSc (Hons) in physics from Imperial College.

Bruce Gardner is a partner in the Financial Services Group, where he specialises in a wide variety of financial services transactions, including formation and promotion of on and offshore funds, drafting and negotiation of documentation between market professionals (such as clearing and settlement arrangements), disciplinary and regulatory issues and corporate transactions for investment industry clients. Bruce's recent experience includes advising in relation to a US$300 million Bermuda-based private equity fund; advising in relation to internet-based securities dealing and clearing arrangements with a number of counterparties including Abbey National, Merrill Lynch and Norwich Union; advising on the structure of a number of retail and institutional funds (including hedge funds); advising in relation to internet-based derivatives trading arrangements; and advising an international bank in relation to regulatory issues at board level.

Richard R. Lindsey is a senior managing director of Bear, Stearns & Co. Inc., where he serves on the firm's Board of Directors, the Operations Committee, the Principal Activities Committee, the Wealth Management Services Advisory Committee, President's Advisory Council, and is Chairman of both the Client Review Committee and the Best Execution Committee. In addition to his responsibilities at Bear Stearns, Richard is the vice chairman of the Board of Directors of the Options Clearing Corporation and is Chairman of the International Association of Financial Engineers. He has a BS in chemical engineering from Illinois Institute of Technology, an MS in chemical engineering from Berkeley, an MBA from the University of Dallas, and a PhD in finance from the University of California, Berkeley.

Karrie H. McMillan is a partner in the Corporate and Financial Services Department of Willkie Farr & Gallagher LLP in Washington DC. Her practice includes advising on on-site examinations and on corporate governance matters and serving as counsel to registered investment companies, their advisers and to alternative investment products managers. Karrie served in positions of increasing responsibility on the staff of the US Securities and Exchange Commission's Division of Investment Management and, as assistant chief counsel of the Division's Office of Chief Counsel, oversaw the development of a number of key interpretive positions on matters involving the investment management industry. She is a member of the Texas and District of Columbia Bar Associations.

Robert Mirsky is leading Deloitte's hedge fund services practice and is responsible for bringing together a cross service line team to serve Deloitte's hedge fund clients and the UK hedge fund marketplace. He has expertise in the structuring and ongoing activities of both start-up hedge funds and global industry giants. Robert joined Deloitte London from the Deloitte Cayman Islands firm where he built and lead that firm's international tax practice focusing on the hedge fund industry. His experience has included international strategic planning, advice and representation with major US accounting firms in New York, Washington, D.C., Milan and Bangkok. Robert received a degree in political science from Boston University and a law degree from American University in Washington, DC.

ACKNOWLEDGEMENTS

The authors and the editor wish to acknowledge the advice and special efforts of the following persons, without whom this book might not have been possible: Neil Roylance, Threadneedle Investments; Andrew Hougie, Dechert LLP; Ken Branson, Mike Hartwell, Eric Janowak and Quentin Johnson of Deloitte; Eric Goldstein, Benjamin Allensworth, Michael Ponder and Jennifer Sullentrip of Willkie Farr & Gallagher LLP.

Hedge Funds: What are They, How are Unregulated Hedge Funds Regulated and How do They View the Hedge Fund–Prime Broker Relationship?

Mark Berman

Editor, SEC Regulation Outside the US

INTRODUCTION

There are more than 10,000 of them. Worldwide, they have assets of US$1.5 trillion.[1] It has been said of them that they are "a major source of liquidity and can significantly enhance market efficiency".[2] They first emerged in the late 1940s.[3] They are companies and limited partnerships. They are established in "offshore" jurisdictions and are "unregulated". Some of them are listed. They do not have executive officers or employees, and rely on others – investment managers, administrators, accountants, lawyers and investment banks/commercial banks – to provide them with the basic services that they require to operate. They make, and lose, significant amounts of money. They draw considerable press and regulatory scrutiny. Unlike market phenomena that come and go, like the "Internet Bubble" of the late 1990s, they have been a constant and integral part of the world's markets. They are both understood and unfathomable. Yet, despite many efforts and a desire to be able to do so, *no one has been able to define what they are.*

They are hedge funds.

This book is devoted to the relationship between hedge funds and prime brokers. It explores what a hedge fund is and is not, analyses the role of prime brokers in the US and elsewhere in the world, surveys the role of hedge fund service providers, explores what comprises a prime brokerage agreement, discusses the trading and economic aspects of this relationships and ends with a summary of key tax, accounting and audit considerations.

Today, the prime broker is one of the most important service providers to a hedge fund, the others being the investment manager and the administrator. Future editions of this book will no doubt cast a different eye on the current shape of the hedge fund–prime brokerage relationship, and other books in this series will deal with each of the other three main "parties" involved with hedge funds.

Hedge funds can be single entity vehicles or master–feeder structures and, occasionally, are listed on exchanges such as the Irish Stock Exchange ("ISE"), the Luxembourg Stock Exchange and the Cayman Islands Stock Exchange – not to mention the Singapore Stock Exchange, the Hong Kong Stock Exchange and other exchanges. They are incorporated in offshore jurisdictions including the Cayman Islands, the British Virgin Islands, Bermuda and Mauritius – are there are signs that other jurisdictions will, in future, become home to even more numbers of hedge funds, notable among them being Jersey and Guernsey.

This chapter discusses what hedge funds are, summarises how "unregulated" hedge funds are regulated, explores what comprises the hedge fund–prime broker relationship and notes how this relationship has changed since hedge fund first signed prime brokerage agreements ("PBAs").

WHAT IS A HEDGE FUND?
What is the difference between a hedge fund and a long only fund?
A hedge fund and a "long only" fund (this includes open-end and closed-end funds, known round the world by many names including mutual funds, investment trusts, unit trusts, OEICs, UCITS, SICAVs and SICAFs, among others)[4] have elements in common. Both, eg, have funds under management ("AUM" or "NAV"), strike a net asset value per share ("NAV per Share") and invest shareholders' money in a pool of instruments. Both may be listed and have to comply with requirements imposed by the listing authority. Both rely on third-party service providers.

There are features that distinguish a hedge fund from a long only fund. These include the fact that the former is largely an investment of choice of institutional investors, including tax paying and tax exempt investors, whereas the former attracts primarily retail investors. Hedge funds are registered in certain jurisdictions and achieve an exchange listing, through which they achieve "light touch" regulation (as discussed below), are able to shield their income from taxation (by virtue of the tax laws of the countries where they are incorporated) and, through listing, become "liquid investments" and attract institution and pension money (that have caps placed on the amount of funds that they may invest in illiquid instruments). This is the case, for example, with hedge funds that are registered in the Cayman Islands with the Cayman Islands Monetary Authority ("CIMA") and that are ISE listed. In other instances, hedge funds are not so registered or listed and are not regulated. By contrast, long only funds marketed primarily to retail investors require formal registration/authorisation and are subject to more stringent regulation. The investment objectives, policies and restrictions that are imposed on hedge funds come from the hedge fund's Articles of Association ("Articles"), local requirements, offering memoranda and, if applicable, listing rules. Long only funds must satisfy numerous requirements in order to achieve and retain authorisation and listing, and must invest within carefully defined parameters that, with the exception of developments such as the UCITS III legislation in Europe, forbid short selling, borrowing to buy and the use of leverage.

Ultimately, what distinguishes a hedge fund from a long only fund? Leverage. Leverage, as used in this book, includes selling short, borrowing to purchase or finance securities and other instruments and using derivatives to enhance returns. Save for UCITS III and by regulatory requirements, long only funds cannot use leverage. Hedge funds, by contrast, and with the exception of certain hedge funds that use a long-only event driven strategy or avoid leverage in market-particular instances (explained elsewhere in this chapter), rely on leverage.

Hedge funds are not private equity investment vehicles
Private equity investment may be broadly defined to include any form of investment that is made on an equity basis and that is not public – ie, it is not exchange listed or traded. Private equity investments commonly take many forms, the most prominent of which

are venture and growth capital investments, buyout funds and mezzanine capital.

Private equity funds differ from hedge funds in several respects. Private equity funds require a fixed term investment, often for a period of up to five years, whereas hedge funds permit investors to redeem their shares or interests (there usually is a fee for redemptions taking place in the first two six month periods, which may be waived by the directors "for good reason"). Next, private equity funds have narrow investment objectives, often for a single purpose. Third, private equity funds operate with a different fee base. Whereas hedge funds have a management fee/performance fee charging structure (ranges are 1–2% for the management fee and 10–20% for performance fees), private equity funds exact a management fee of a stated per cent for the investment period (these would range from 2 through 5%, possibly higher) and a per cent of the invested capital after the stated investment period ended, plus a performance fee after calculation of the IRR hurdle. Fourth, investment in a private equity fund takes place at the beginning of the investment term, and the investors usually engage in extensive negotiations of documentation prior to close, whereas hedge funds usually experience continuous periods of subscription and redemptions and, save for occasional side letters (to the extent that they are issued), documents are not negotiated.

Despite these differences, there are some areas where hedge funds and private equity investment vehicles, or their investments, have come together, or where hedge funds themselves have joined forces to achieve desired results.[5]

Hedge fund managers, as they attempt to generate higher returns, have begun to invest in "hybrid" funds. Hedge funds have also sought to further leverage their returns by investing in acquisitions[6] and, in certain instances, have joined forces with other hedge funds or with private equity investment vehicles as bidders or to force corporate changes. The most notable of these were the February 2006 joint unsolicited offer by Soros Fund Management, LLC, Atticus Capital LP ("Atticus") and Almeida Oil Co., Inc. for the reorganisation of Star Gas Partners LP[7] and the efforts in May 2005 of the Children's Investment Fund Management, Atticus and others to object to the bid by Deutsche Börse for the London Stock Exchange and the subsequent resignation of Deutsche Börse chairman Rolff Breuer.[8] In September 2006, it was reported that two hedge funds had served notice on Stork to discuss the sale of that company's divisions and that they were both encouraging Royal Ahold to sell certain of its US businesses.[9]

It has not been all "one way" movement, as private equity investment vehicles have established their own hedge funds.

Can and should "hedge fund" be defined?

Hedge funds are sold to investors in dozens of jurisdictions. The more than 10,000 hedge funds that are reputed to be in existence (this figure does not include now closed hedge funds) have under investment more than US$1.5 trillion. They account for significant trading volume in listed securities and are significant players in the over the counter ("OTC") market, figures that have increased almost exponentially in the last few years. Hedge funds generate considerable amounts of commission for the brokerage firms with whom they effect transactions. They also generate handsome, even significant, profits for prime brokers, the entities on whom hedge funds rely for their funding.

Does there exist today a definition of the term "hedge fund"? Is it necessary to define "hedge fund"? Is it true that "hedge funds are notoriously difficult to define"?[10]

In its March 2006 consultation paper, "The Regulatory Environment for Hedge Funds: A Survey and Comparison" (March 2006)[11], the International Organization of Securities Commissions ("IOSCO") provided a survey of the current state of hedge fund regulation on a global basis. The IOSCO paper also surveyed the regulatory requirements imposed on the sale of shares and interests in hedge funds in several jurisdictions and the requirements imposed on the investment managers that advise hedge funds. Strikingly, the IOSCO paper found that there is no jurisdiction that defines a hedge fund in its operative laws, rules and regulations.

This is not to say that regulators have not attempted to define this special type of investment vehicle. In the SEC Hedge Fund Study and in its 2004 release[12] adopting Rule 203(b)(3)-2 and amending other rules under the US Investment Advisers Act of 1940 ("Advisers Act"), the SEC defined "hedge fund" as any pooled investment vehicle that is privately organised, administered by professional investment managers, and not widely available to the public.[13] The UK Financial Services Authority ("FSA") in recent consultation papers defined hedge funds "as any pooled investment vehicle that is privately organised, administered by professional investment managers, and not widely available to the public", and referred to the fact that "the term can be defined by considering the characteristics most commonly associated with hedge funds".[14] Many other regulators have issued consultation papers not just on the structure of hedge funds, but on the role that they play and on the risks that they pose.

Hedge funds have drawn scrutiny in hearings before the US Congress and other legislative bodies world-wide. In testimony before the US Congress, SEC Chairman Christopher Cox said that hedge funds provide "tangible benefits" and "contribute substantially to capital formation, market efficiency, price discovery, and liquidity", but that there is "[t]he potential for retail investors to be harmed by hedge fund risk" and that there is a "lack of ... basic data" about hedge funds.[15] A report published by the Autoriteit Financiële Markten, the Dutch regulator, stated that a lack of transparency was a concern and that it was not clear whether managers had a sufficient understanding of their hedge fund's investment policies and risk profiles, but that hedge funds did contribute to the markets by providing liquidity.[16] The topic attracts academic scrutiny and examination. Yet, hedge funds continue to play a significant, positive role in the world's securities and derivatives markets.

Although they do not do it directly, regulators indirectly define hedge funds in the manner in which they impose controls on investment managers that advise hedge funds and on prime brokers that fund and provide other services (*see* chapter 3) to hedge funds. Also, exchanges do this when they provide in their listing rules provisions to permit hedge funds to be listed.

Yet, despite attracting considerable regulatory scrutiny, no defin ition of hedge fund has been enshrined into law.

Is it important to define hedge fund? Is it necessary to do so?

The issue of trying to define the term "hedge fund" is connected to the issue of whether hedge funds should be regulated, which is explored below.

For now, and for purposes of this book, we will define a hedge fund as a collective investment vehicle that receives funds from its investors (including institutions, pension funds and high net worth individuals) and invests those monies using one or more strategies, with or without leverage, in order to achieve a profit or absolute return.

WHAT ARE HEDGE FUNDS?
Single entity hedge funds and master–feeder structures
Hedge funds are usually limited partnerships, companies or limited liability companies. The limited partnership model, where the general partner serves as investment manager and administrator (or delegates these roles), is used primarily in the US. In this model, investors become limited partners, not shareholders.

Establishing a hedge fund as a company is the form that is used primarily outside the US. In the company model, investors purchase shares in the hedge fund directly or, if the hedge fund is established as a master–feeder structure, in a feeder fund. Returns are realised at the time of the redemption of shares. Dividends in any form are rarely declared and paid.

Hedge funds take one of two structures: single entity funds and feeder funds.

In a single entity fund, Figure 1, investors invest directly in the hedge fund itself. The hedge fund invests those funds directly in

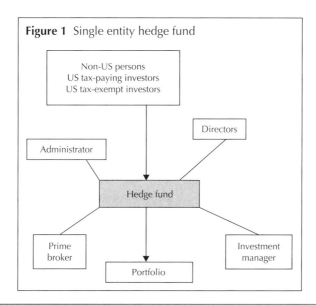

Figure 1 Single entity hedge fund

the portfolio comprised of securities, derivatives, cash and other instruments. The hedge fund (or its general partner) contracts directly with the investment manager, the administrator, the prime broker and other service providers. The general partner or directors of single entity funds are responsible for all aspects of governance, operation and oversight, and delegate under strict contractual provisions aspects of operations and control to the service providers.

Single entity hedge funds attract investments from non-US persons and US persons – including both tax-paying investors and tax-exempt investors. Single entity hedge funds provide a simple structure within which to work, but this may lead to complications for the investors involved – primarily for US investors. US tax-paying investors in corporate funds may find that they have invested in a passive foreign company ("PFIC") and would suffer adverse tax consequences. Such investors may wish to make the "qualified fund election" ("QEF") to avoid adverse tax consequences, which is discussed in more detail in Chapter 8.

A master–feeder structure provides a means to address the PFIC issue present in a single entity hedge fund but it raises issues that are generally not relevant to single entity funds. US tax-exempt investors and non-US investors purchase shares in the "offshore feeder fund". Offshore feeder funds are usually companies that are incorporated, or partnerships that are organised, in the so-called "offshore jurisdictions" such as the Cayman Islands, Jersey and other countries. US tax-paying investors buy membership interests ("Interests") in the "onshore feeder fund" or the master fund. Onshore feeder funds are usually Delaware limited liability companies or limited partnerships. Each feeder fund invests all or substantially all of its assets – investors' funds – in the "master fund" which, in turn, holds the portfolio. Examples of feeder funds are illustrated in Figures 2 and 3.

Master–feeders are structures that are more complicated than single entity funds. There are multiple companies to manage, multiple boards of directors or general partners, additional and more complex agreements to have in place, a need to coordinate subscriptions, redemptions and exchanges to ensure the correct proportion of investment per class (and sub-class, if present) in the feeder funds and in the master fund and multiple layers of monitoring, oversight and control. There are tax issues, as well.

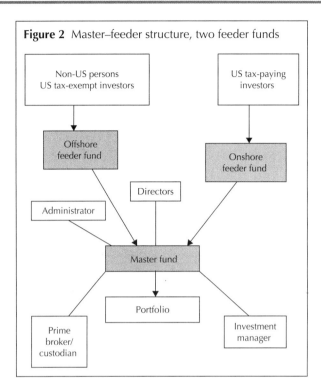

Figure 2 Master–feeder structure, two feeder funds

Master–feeder structures were established primarily to suit the requirements of US investors. The master–feeder structure permits US tax-paying investors to invest without PFIC issues. It helps US tax-exempt investors, if they invest in the offshore feeder fund, to avoid unrelated business tax income ("UBTI"). It does require that any onshore feeder fund and the master fund elect to be treated as a partnership for US tax purposes in order to be able to pass through the tax benefits to US tax-paying investors.

Hedge funds globally

Hedge funds are established as a single entity or as a master–feeder structure. However, the model differs from one region of the world to another.

In the European model, which often involves Cayman Island private companies (rather than partnerships) as single entity funds or master–feeder structures, the fund, the investment manager, the

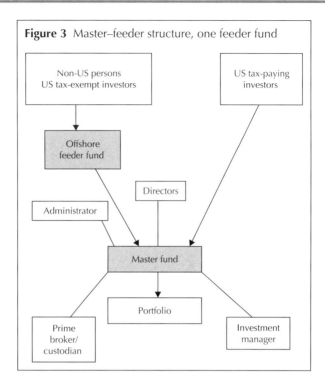

Figure 3 Master–feeder structure, one feeder fund

administrator and the fund and the prime broker(s) are independent from each other. The directors of the hedge fund exercise independent oversight over the service providers. This model helps minimise conflicts of interest and ensures that problems with valuations are timely and properly addressed.

In the Asian model, which usually features a company (or, for certain markets, notably Japan, a unit trust) but may also be based on the partnership model, there is an "onshore" manager that handles certain administrative matters while an "offshore" manager serves as the investment manager.

In the American model, and to accommodate relevant tax, legal and regulatory requirements, hedge funds are structured as limited partnerships with a single entity – the general partner – performing multiple roles – general partner, investment manager and administrator. Investors are limited partners. Occasionally, hedge funds are established as limited liability companies or as business trusts.[17]

The American model, like the European and Asian models, evolved from, or were developed to take advantage of "loopholes" in, local legal, tax and regulatory requirements. Unlike the European model, however, the presence in this model of a single entity performing multiple roles may not provide the type of safeguards to address or to prevent conflicts of interest or valuation problems. This was evident in *SEC v Beacon Hill*,[18] which involved, *inter alia*, the investment manager/sponsor, Beacon Hill Asset Management, LLC ("Beacon Hill"), misrepresenting the method used to value investments in the master fund's portfolio and manipulating the manner in which the NAVs of the funds that it managed were calculated. According to the Amended Complaint filed by the SEC against Beacon Hill, the prime broker of the hedge funds that Beacon Hill managed, Bear Stearns, questioned the portfolio valuations, "insisted that Beacon Hill address the apparent and substantial discrepancy in the net value of the Master Fund"[19] and, when no action was taken, notified the SEC of the discrepancy in the valuations of the portfolio and stated its concern over the discrepancy.[20] *Beacon Hill* is thus an example of both how a single entity assumes multiple functions and, unfortunately, gets it wrong, and how a prime broker rightly queries portfolio valuations and acts when appropriate clarification and rectification is not forthcoming.

Service providers

Apart from necessary governance activities by the directors or the general partner, hedge funds rely on service providers for their activities (*see* Figure 4). The key service providers to hedge funds are the administrator, the investment manager and the prime broker(s). Other service providers are the distributor, listing sponsor (if the fund or one of the feeder funds is listed), legal counsel, company secretary, money laundering reporting officer ("MLRO"), auditors, executing brokers, trading counterparties, hardware and software providers, risk managers and custodians or transfer agents that are independent of the prime broker. (Occasionally, and in a manner that would not raise taxation or corporate governance issues, the company secretarial and MLRO role may be performed by one service provider other than the investment manager or the prime broker.) All operate under the oversight of the directors

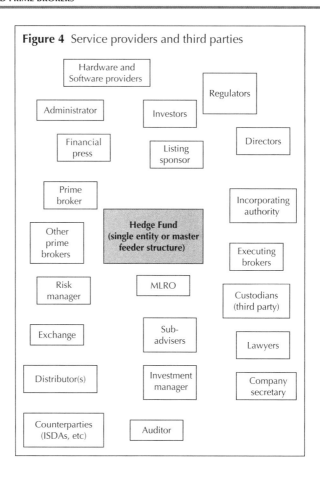

Figure 4 Service providers and third parties

(or the general partner). Third party entities that are involved include the investors, regulators, any exchange where the hedge fund is listed and tax and governmental authorities. The roles of service providers in relation to the hedge funds are discussed in Chapter 4.

The investment manager contracts directly with the fund, or the master fund in a master–feeder structure. (The general partner performs this rule in the US LLP structure.) It manages the portfolio on a fully discretionary basis in compliance with the investment management agreement between it and the hedge fund/master fund, its own regulatory requirements, the hedge fund's offering materials (a prospectus or private placement memorandum for single entity hedge funds, or the prospectus and the private placement memorandum for the offshore feeder fund and the onshore feeder fund, respectively, in a master–feeder structure)[21] and exchange requirements, if the hedge fund is listed. This includes managing the portfolio, instructing executing brokers to effect transactions, liaising with investors when queries arise about aspects of the portfolio, attending meetings of the directors or the general partner and answering queries on reports, and other matters expressly stated in the Investment Management Agreement ("IMA"). Investment managers do not price individual positions or portfolios (but may provide information to the administrator to help it perform this function), do not select, add, subtract or replace service providers (but may provide advice), do not take decisions or make recommendations to the directors or general partner (in order to avoid having the hedge fund be taxed in the jurisdiction where the investment manager is located eg, the UK), do not accept or reject investors and do not exercise oversight over the other service providers (this is a role that is to be performed by the directors or the general partner).

The administrator values positions, handles subscriptions, redemptions and exchanges, calculates the NAV and the NAV per Share, corresponds with investors, manages aspects of the annual audit and provides monitoring services. It signs an Administration Agreement with the hedge fund or the feeder funds and the master fund (or the general partner) in a master–feeder structure.

The PBA, annexes of or other documents related to the PBA and the disclosures in the Offering Materials establish, define and govern the relationship between hedge fund and prime broker(s). In a single entity structure, the prime broker contracts with the hedge fund. In a master–feeder structure, only the master fund and not a feeder fund sign the PBA. Chapter 5 of this book explores the legal documents that govern the relationship, including a non-US PBA, in detail, while Chapters 2 and 3 treat the legal relationship from the US perspective and the commercial relationship from the industry perspective, respectively.

THE HEDGE FUND–PRIME BROKERAGE RELATIONSHIP

The hedge fund–prime broker relationship is shaped by a number of documents, legal requirements imposed on the prime brokers and the investment managers, on commercial and market forces – and on the need to deliver absolute return to investors. Ultimately, the prime broker-hedge fund relationship comes down to simple matters: funding; stock borrowing; seed capital; custody services; and capital introduction programmes. No prime broker would provide only funding: if this were the case, the directors or the general partner of the hedge fund would, in short order, secure a second prime broker or change prime brokers.[22]

Hedge funds emerged at a time when the world's securities markets were in the first stages of internationalisation. At this, time and during the 1970s and 1980s, investment banks and commercial banks were running newly formed stock borrowing and lending desks and expanding their custodial networks, globally (directly or through affiliations). Increasingly, investors were purchasing securities on margin and, in the early and mid 1970s, beginning to understand the role of options not just to hedge, but to trade for profit. In jurisdictions that permitted it, short selling[23] was becoming a feature of portfolio management (apart from being a tool of market makers). Then, unlike today, there were three distinct "markets": securities; commodities; and derivatives. The commoditisation of the securities market and the growth of the derivatives markets, exchange-traded and OTC, began to blur the distinctions between these three markets, started to link them, paved the way for the development of more exotic instruments and vehicles and provided more "arrows in the quiver" for investment managers. The quest for enhanced returns had begun. By using securities, futures on commodities and derivatives alone or in strategies, and with the growth of dynamic hedging and the search for "alpha",[24] hedge funds were able to offer institutional investors and high net worth retail investors a means to achieve "absolute return" – ie, to achieve gains in both bull and bear markets[25]. Hedge funds became a force in the 1980s and, on the back of thriving markets and increased returns, became a recognised niche player in the world's markets in the 1990s. In the early 2000s, and after the collapse of the Internet Bubble and the re-emergence of banks into the securities markets (caused by the repeal of the Glass-Steagall Act brought about by the Gramm-Leach-Bliley Act), hedge funds sought and thrived on volatility, expanded dramatically in numbers and swelled in terms of AUM. Trading volumes, hedge fund borrowings to fund trading and prime broker lending (and financing to fund this lending) increased. There were, to be sure, near disasters such as Long-Term Capital Management. Instances of fraud, insider trading and manipulation were attributed to unscrupulous investment managers and hedge fund directors and investors. Overall, however, hedge funds continued to play a valuable role in the world's markets and rose from niche player to the first rank, a role they occupy today. One might even say that hedge funds have "arrived" – and point to Moody's assigning its first hedge fund operations quality rating to Sorin Capital Management, LLC.[26]

Hedge funds could not have secured their toe-hold and evolved from niche player to first rank without prime brokers. By the same token, in the early 1970s, commercial and investment banks as prime brokers could not have envisaged the rise of hedge funds into an industry that, today, accounts for a significant part of their operations, trading and custodial activity, income and profits. Hedge funds and prime brokers sought each other out, grew and matured together and, like ying and yang, "baseball, hot dogs and apple pie" and "Morecambe and Wise", have become nearly inseparable partners on the world economic stage.

When hedge funds emerged, the commercial and investment banks that became their prime brokers did not have ready-to-use precedent PBAs, as is the case today. Hedge funds in start-up mode sought prime brokers primarily for their funding, stock borrowing and custodial requirements. Commercial and investment banks had hedge funds execute stock borrowing and lending agreements, terms to buy securities on margin, standard account opening terms and conditions and ISDAs and other agreements to buy and sell derivatives, repos and other OTC instruments. At the time, regulatory requirements in major jurisdictions did not envisage the existence of hedge funds or their growth and emergence as a market force. Differences in market conditions drove different types of investment, investment strategies and structures of hedge funds. There gradually emerged two types of PBA: the American model, shaped by a 1994 SEC no-action letter (*see* Chapter 2) and the global model, which in one form or another is used outside the US (provisions of which are analysed in Chapter 5).

PBAs are today written agreements that define and govern key aspects of the relationship: credit; events of default; security interest, termination; trading oversight and the cost and terms of funding. The PBAs that were used in the early days of the relationship resembled, from a credit, security interest, default and termination standpoint, agreements that minimised risk for the prime brokers. In large part, they shifted risk almost entirely to the hedge fund. It would be impolite to say that early PBAs helped to define the hedge fund–prime broker relationship on a borrower-lender basis, but in large part this was not far from the truth. Many provisions of PBAs were then and, in some instances, are today, one sided and favour the prime broker. Early in the relationship, prime brokers rarely negotiated PBAs. (ISDAs were negotiated but continued to reflect key terms that preserved the credit superiority of the prime broker, such as NAV triggers, key man provisions and material changes, as additional termination events.) The central arguments given then, and now, are that hedge funds are seekers (and prime brokers providers) of credit, that prime brokers provide services to many hedge funds at one time and need consistency in the terms of their agreements to comply with their own legal and regulatory requirements and ensure efficient operations and that prime brokers knew the market and what was best for the nascent hedge fund.

Prime brokers were thus, in the first instance, providers of credit. They are effectively this today, but on different terms and in different ways. Indeed, they are moving quickly to be able to offer enhanced services to hedge funds by offering capital introduction ("cap intro") programmes and multi-functional electronic platforms that permit, eg, multi-strategy trading in different asset classes and currencies, and that allows a hedge fund to work with more than one prime broker.[27] Multiple prime brokers may almost be a requirement for certain hedge funds. According to a report published by Paladyne Systems LLC, "The Need for Multi-Prime Brokers",[28] increased industry demand and changing investor needs will require hedge funds that achieve certain large AUMs and that depend increasingly on technology to use multiple prime brokers.

What factors are changing the relationship?

The factors are competition, market volatility (or the lack of volatility and the need to squeeze returns by using increasingly sophisticated instruments and trading strategies), the regulation of service providers, investors' demand for increasing returns, shareholder activism, market forces and, simply, more hedge funds. A hedge fund needs to earn enough not only to cover the management and performance fees owed to the investment manager and fees to service providers, but to a suitable return to investors. The demand by investors for better returns translates into a need to cut costs and margins. The increasing sophistication of directors leads to stronger oversight, tough controls and better and well negotiated documentation. Regulators are scrutinising hedge funds and some are calling for them to be regulated.

In an era of intense competition, regulatory scrutiny, decreasing margins and RFP processes to select prime brokers, the simple fact is that if a hedge fund doesn't like one set of terms or if it establishes that its costs are too high, terms are negotiated or costs are lowered, or the directors might consider hiring a second prime broker or taking their business elsewhere.

While it is true that a small number of commercial and investment banks account for a large proportion of hedge fund prime brokerage activity today,[29] the above factors, increasing numbers of banks and brokers seeking to become prime brokers and more hedge firms with a track record seeking best terms with the lowest possible costs are demanding, and receiving, parity in the relationship. Broad definitions of key terms such as act of insolvency and events of default, unequal termination terms, fixed and floating charges over the entire portfolio (not just over the amount of credit actually extended), the unilateral ability to "DK" trades and other "credit required" provisions are no longer automatically accepted in PBAs. NAV decline triggers in ISDAs are no longer an industry standard and "required" for hedge funds. Hedge funds no longer appoint prime brokers and *then* review PBAs. Hedge funds recognise that prime brokers may be just as susceptible to credit risk as they are. Today, competitive RFP processes and a demand for parity mean that the hedge fund–prime broker relationship is closer to or at true level-playing field. For both hedge funds and prime brokers, the relationship is evolving from borrower-lender to partner. These changes are beneficial to both prime broker and hedge fund and, in the long run, will help ensure, from the standpoint of these market participants, orderly markets, sound market players and investor protection.

REGULATING HEDGE FUNDS

Are hedge fund regulated or unregulated? How does one regulate "unregulated" hedge funds? Is it necessary to regulate hedge funds?

The model for our analysis is the European model, which is a single entity hedge fund or a master–feeder structure that is incorporated in the Cayman Islands,[30] has a European-based investment manager, a European (or local subsidiary of a US bank) prime broker, a European (Dublin- or Luxembourg-based) administrator and is listed on the ISE. In certain jurisdictions, hedge funds have obtained a listing. In other jurisdictions, fund of hedge funds are listed.

Hedge funds are not directly regulated as are long only funds, but they are not, for the most part, entirely unregulated. Our model hedge fund is regulated and complies with a number of requirements imposed on it directly by home country licensing authority and the exchange where its shares are listed, and indirectly by the investment manager, the prime broker, the directors and the administrator satisfying requirements imposed on them as regards their clients and their activities.

The regulator in the hedge fund's home country jurisdiction, such as CIMA in the Cayman Islands, will, on the hedge fund's registration and compliance with certain conditions (continuing obligations), issue it with a license as a regulated mutual fund with CIMA. This fact is stated in the hedge fund's Prospectus or, for certain types of master–feeder structures, the Offering Materials. The conditions for obtaining a license include, *inter alia*, filing an initial prospectus that must "describe the equity interests in all material respects ... and contain such other information as is necessary to enable a prospective investor in the [fund] to make an informed decision as to whether or not to subscribe for or purchase [the shares]",[31] and filing further amendments to that prospectus. Other relevant requirements include imposing a minimum investment unless the fund is listed on a recognised stock exchange (the Cayman Islands Stock Exchange, the ISE or the Luxembourg Bourse),[32] obtaining administrator and auditor consent to hold those positions, naming its directors and MLRO, filing and distributing unaudited periodic returns and to file and distribute audited financial statements. Core fund requirements include satisfying anti-money laundering ("AML") requirements for investors. An important requirement is that CIMA will not grant a license "until it has been satisfied by the applicant that–

(a) each promoter is of sound reputation;
(b) the administration of the mutual fund will be undertaken–

    (i) by persons who have sufficient expertise to administer the mutual fund;
    (ii) by persons who are fit and proper to be directors or, as the case may be, managers or officers in their respective positions; and

(c) the business of the mutual fund and any offer of equity interests in it will be carried out in a proper way." [33]

The listing authority imposes requirements on the hedge fund and on its directors. Typical requirements imposed on a listed hedge fund by the ISE are: compliance with core investment objectives, policies and restrictions and a ban on making changes to these within the first three years of the fund's life without shareholder approval; regular reporting of the NAV; compliance with continuing obligations (eg, developments, material changes in ownership); making timely announcements when material developments take place; filing original and amended prospectuses and material contracts; and complying with the EU Market Abuse Directive to help prevent trading or market-related activities that are manipulative or are based on the misuse of inside information.

As regards the hedge fund's directors, the prospectus filed with the ISE must include a biography of each director, state each individuals other relevant directorships and provide a statement whether any such person has been subject to "bad boy" provisions:

"… any unspent convictions in relation to indictable offences;
… details of any bankruptcies or individual voluntary arrangements of such person;
… details of any receiverships, compulsory liquidations, creditors voluntary liquidations, administrations, company voluntary arrangements or any composition or arrangements with its creditors generally or any class of its creditors of any company where such person was a director with an executive function at the time of or within the 12 months preceding such events;
… details of any compulsory liquidations, administrations or partnership voluntary arrangements of any partnership where such person was a partner at the time of or within the 12 months preceding such events;

... details of receiverships of any asset of such person or of a partnership of which the person was a partner at the time of or within the 12 months preceding such event; and

... details of any public criticisms of such person by statutory or regulatory authorities (including recognised professional bodies) and whether such person has ever been disqualified by a court from acting as a director of a company or from acting in the management or conduct of the affairs of any company

or, if there is no such information to be disclosed, a statement of that fact."[34]

Most hedge fund investment managers are authorised and regulated in at least one jurisdiction (dual registration is rare). The US saw an increase of investment adviser registrations when the SEC adopted Rule 203(b)(3)-2 and amended other rules under the Advisers Act: the number of non-US advisers that registered with the SEC nearly doubled. The *Goldstein* court vacated the rule, but the numbers of registered advisers may not drop sharply due to de-registrations.[35] However, there will certainly be a slow down in the number of new registrations, and certain market participants and trade industry associations are calling for regulators, in particular, the SEC, not to pursue dual registration.

The regulatory (and, if applicable, common law) requirements imposed on regulated investment managers include: complying with account opening and AML requirements; ensuring that written agreements are in place for discretionary management clients that spell out the terms of the relationship; providing best execution; allocation and fair dealing; disclosure of risks for certain classes of instruments (such as options and derivatives); and other key provisions. In the US, provisions of the Advisers Act require, *inter alia*: written policies and procedures reasonably designed to prevent violation of the Advisers Act by the manager or its supervised persons; the annual review of all policies and procedures; the appointment of a qualified compliance officer; procedures to monitor risk and evaluate individual client exposure to certain issuers or sectors; a code of ethics with standards of conduct expected of the manager and its advisory personnel, controls to safeguard information about client transactions and address conflicts that arise from personal trading by advisory personnel, a personal account dealing programme; and compliance with the requirement that agreements be terminable at will (and not on a fixed term basis) and without a termination fee. Investment Management Agreements typically contain provisions that cover: duties and obligations (including best execution, allocation, aggregation and others); procedures for delegation; when proxies may be voted; fund obligations; compliance with restrictions and requirements; fees and expenses, including a statement of how performance fees will be calculated and paid (in coordination with the hedge fund's Offering Materials and Articles); conflicts of interest; risk warnings for certain instruments; market rules; confidentiality obligations; a statement on operational procedures; policies on "bundled and unbundled" brokerage and "soft commissions"; and governing law.

Prime brokers are regulated commercial or investment banks that must comply with certain regulatory requirements as regards their activities for hedge funds. They, too, have account opening and AML requirements. The area or department inside the prime broker handling prime brokerage activities must comply with policies and procedures to ensure the confidentiality of information and trading strategies. The extension of credit and stock lending must be made, monitored and reported per the relevant prudential obligations and consolidated at the parent company level; custodial requirements must be handled pursuant to relevant legal and regulatory obligations; books and records must be kept and maintained; and business continuity plans must be in place. Non-regulatory legal requirements that are imposed on prime brokers include provisions to document and perfect a charge and local market trading and clearing restrictions. Prime brokers that are custodians and that use sub-custodians, affiliated and non-affiliated, or that do not provide custody services but rely on others for this, are subject, directly or indirectly, to many local requirements through authorisations or contractual provisions. They are the first port of call for the hedge fund on issues such as netting, default and insolvency of the local custodians.

These provisions, and others, create a mosaic of legal, regulatory and contractual requirements and controls that affect nearly every aspect of hedge fund activity and operation. Investors such as pension funds and wealthy individuals do not wish to risk substantial amounts of money, prime brokers would not engage in business to expose themselves and their employees to liability, investment managers would not trade portfolios absent controls and risk enforcement action and the loss of their authorisation and individuals would not serve as directors in an environment absent proper controls and compliance with legal and regulatory requirements.

There are, to be sure, hedge funds that are not listed and that have a portfolio that is managed by an entity that engages in business in reliance on an exemption from regulation. Such hedge funds may not have a prime broker and may rely, instead, on their own network of custodians and executing brokers with which to trade, borrow funds and securities.

For the most part, however, the model hedge fund is subject to light touch regulation, as evidenced by home country requirements such as those of the Jersey Financial Services Commission and the Cayman Mutual Fund Laws. The degree of regulation increases if the hedge fund obtains a listing. The level of regulation is also effected by controls and requirements placed on service providers and by investors "voting with their feet": if one does not like what it sees, one will redeem its shares.

Should hedge funds be regulated? In many ways they already are regulated and in other aspects they are not. Regulators cite, with validity, many reasons why hedge funds should be regulated:

❑ to prevent fraud;
❑ when shares or interests are sold to non-institutional investors, to provide full and fair disclosure of all relevant matters;
❑ to ensure transparency in valuations and proper valuation methods;
❑ to help prevent market abuse (manipulation and insider trading);
❑ to provide a safety net to avoid or help prevent systemic risk;
❑ to gain information about the trading and operational habits of hedge funds, their managers and prime brokers to ensure orderly markets and to obtain sufficient information to identify, understand and address the risks raised by hedge funds.

At the same time, regulators have found that hedge funds can, eg, "significantly enhance market efficiency",[36] "serve as an important took for investors by providing valuable portfolio diversification"[37] and "assume risks by serving as ready counterparties to entities that wish to hedge risk".[38]

DO HEDGE FUNDS POSE RISKS?

Some hedge funds are not listed or not CIMA or otherwise approved and may operate under a cloak of invisibility, in an effort not only to avoid regulation but, possibly, to shelter positions and strategies from investors. The hedge funds that are listed or are held by pension plans and other institutional investors are managed by regulated investment managers, funded by authorised prime brokers and offer their securities in reliance on Offering Materials that state the investment objective, policies and restrictions (which may be changed only by a shareholder approval). These hedge funds are required to publish annual reports with information about positions and profits and, because they are listed, must comply with exchange-imposed positions disclosure. The prime brokers and administrators of such funds monitor positions and require disclosure to regulatory authorities of large positions – 3% in the UK and Germany (from January 1, 2007) and 5% in the US. It would not be true to say that all or the majority of hedge funds "remain secretive about their positions and strategies, even to their own investors".[39] If this was truly the case, legitimate money in hedge funds would soon disappear, prime brokers would contract only with authorised and listed hedge funds and investment managers would cease managing hedge fund portfolios.

Hedge funds trade to achieve absolute returns, aside from event driven funds that take positions to become a catalyst for change. Investment managers must achieve profits sufficient to cover not only their management fee/performance fee but to provide a return to investors.

Poor returns translate into redemptions. Small portfolios generate lower returns and require more concerted efforts and increased leverage to extract profit. This may strain investment and hedging strategies and lead to trading on the edge, or in violation, of investment objectives and policies. Redemptions may also lead to more redemptions and a cascade effect that, if precipitous and in the presence of NAV triggers as additional termination events in ISDAs, might result in the liquidation of positions and, possibly, cross defaults, bringing a PBA into an event of details and possibly closing the hedge fund.

Leverage permits a hedge fund to achieve returns greater than by trading merely to outperform standard benchmarks or to invest directly in instruments. Leverage, to a hedge fund, is not just selling short or borrowing, but utilising complex and sometimes interlocking trading strategies over combinations of purchases and sales of investments, simple and complex, liquid and illiquid, that generate enhanced return. The instruments that help to achieve this are loan participations, collateralised debt obligations ("CDOs"), collateralised loan obligations ("CLOs"), collateralised bond obligations ("CBOs"), repos, swaps, exchange traded funds ("ETFs"), credit derivatives, credit default swaps ("CDS"), contracts for differences ("CFDs"), OTC derivatives, futures, warrants, options and warrants, special purpose vehicles ("SPVs") over securities, derivatives, loan participations, indices and other instruments that exist or that are created to achieve a desired effect – individually or in combinations. Value needs to be derived not just from each strategy, but from each instrument in a portfolio. In a sudden market movement, to generate cash to handle large redemptions or in the event of a need to rebalance a portfolio, it may be sufficient to simply buy or sell instruments or to unwind parts of a strategy or hedge, or to sell portfolio insurance. It may, however, become necessary to sell core positions. It is not always possible to sell the assets that lie at the core of multiple trading, investment and hedging strategies, to obtain a price, to sell them quickly or to settle them quickly and realise cash flows (extended settlements draw penalties from demanding, uncompromising counterparties). This is a function of the liquidity of the asset, and examples of this are loan participations and exotic OTC structures. Thus, illiquid assets, which help generate leverage, may lead to the risk of unsellable instruments or imbalanced portfolios.

Another risk is regulation. Regulators or tax authorities may change laws or regulations, resulting in changes to the treatment of positions and the need to alter requirements or portfolios. Trading to avoid regulation is another risk. Trading CFDs in the UK to avoid buying exchange-traded equities to avoid stamp duty or stamp duty reserve tax may, if done with incorrect documentation or in extraordinary volumes or complex transactions, draw regulatory scrutiny and result in the imposition of assessments, interest charges and penalties.

Leveraging returns involves elements of avoiding or hedging risk, achieving cash returns and realising enhanced returns. In an effort to trade to generate increased returns and to find and profit on inconsistencies in the pricing of instruments, spreads or funding gaps – and to keep investors – managers look to extract value from nearly any source. Doing so involves the shifting of risk from one portfolio to another. Value can be derived from nearly any asset. So, too, can leverage, but spreads and leverage are small when liquid, exchange traded securities are involved.

According to the SEC, hedge funds "assume risks by serving as ready counterparties to entities that wish to hedge risk".[40] One such risk is credit risk. The credit derivatives market is growing, exponentially. A prime driver of this market is not the investment or commercial bank that structures the derivative to remove credit risk from the balance sheet of the industrial company (and receives a fee) or the company that wishes to shed it, but the investor that is seeking increased returns and the hedge funds that offer this to investors and that trade this risk – and the prime brokers that fund such trading (and receive fees). Since the end of the "Internet Bubble", trading volumes, prime broker borrowing and lending, financing to fund such borrowing and pending and other market indicators have increased significantly. Inflation has remained at a relatively constant "low rate". Against these and other economic, regulatory and political factors, the credit derivatives market has grown on an accelerated basis. The shift of credit risk has accelerated: in some cases, credit risk has moved from the balance sheet of the industrial company to and through commercial and investment banks – in some cases, prime brokers – to hedge funds. Someone has to come up with the cash in the event that a payment is required under a credit derivative. A single industrial company going into insolvency may not cause hedge funds and/or prime brokers world-wide to fail – systemic risk. A slow down in the credit derivatives market, a recession or other event that triggers defaults in credit derivatives and requires large payments may, however, cause more than one large hedge fund that might not have readily available cash to make a payment to liquidate part of a portfolio and, at the same time, cover redemptions and, possibly, margin calls. A slowdown in the credit derivatives market might result in the commercial and investment banks that package credit derivatives for sale and that fund hedge fund purchases of these instruments receiving lower commissions and fees, experiencing reduced trading, seeing hedge funds with multiple prime brokers trading away from them and even losing favoured hedge fund clients. Hedge funds might become insurers via credit derivatives and the shift of risk to them, and have to pay large amounts of money. This might result in smaller portfolios and more pressure to generate returns with increased leverage and lower returns which may lead to further redemptions – or the need to trade "at the edge" or to influence valuations. Such a cycle, one started, might be hard to control.

In the European model, valuations are done by the administrator under the supervision of the directors, not under the control of investment manager. In the American model, however, and as evidenced by *Beacon Hill*, the general partner of a limited liability partnership hedge fund that is the investment manager may do, control or influence valuations. The risk here is to ensure that valuations are conducted in a transparent manner by an independent party, free from the risk of influence, and to ensure that prices of underlying instruments are independently verifiable and not dependent on estimates or "unverifiable" prices.

IS IT NECESSARY TO REGULATE HEDGE FUNDS?

As noted above, there are risks associated with hedge funds and with prime brokers. There are risks in the markets that are not associated with either of these. Hedge funds and prime brokers, alone and together, play a valuable role in our markets. To impose levels or types of regulation without careful consideration may change the dynamics in such a way so as to change or harm the very markets that we are trying to protect. To the extent that risk is identified and managed, a hedge fund and a prime broker may be subject to reduced risk. However, and in a global market where players use the internet to trade large positions with increasing amounts of borrowed funds and securities, risk becomes diffused. It may be unavoidable that a hedge fund becomes insolvent and, with it, a prime broker. Three prime brokers share more than 50% of the world hedge fund market. To have one of these prime brokers go insolvent is disconcerting. It is unavoidable that some level of new, or additional, regulation will be imposed. Hedge funds are not, however, long only funds that are incorporated in mainstream jurisdictions and are largely offered to retail investors. It may be argued, persuasively, that the current level and type of regulation discussed above, with certain demonstrated additional provisions placed not on hedge funds alone *but also on the service providers*, would suffice and address the risks noted above, and others. What is required is information to be able to understand the risks that arise from hedge fund activity, to understand the dramatic growth in trading patterns, funding and derivatives markets (eg, credit derivatives).

What might be done?

Transaction reports by executing brokers and prime brokers should be tagged to provide trading activity that would help identify hedge fund trading. It would not be necessary to define the term hedge fund, but indicators could be used that would define other, similar types of entities that would lead to a tag to help exchanges and regulators, with vast information sharing mechanisms, see trading patters emerge not just in one market (geographical or product) but across markets.

Dual regulation of investment managers is duplicative, costly and potentially ineffective, but coordinated regulation and information sharing is beneficial. The SEC's adoption in 2004 of Rule 203(b)(3)-2 and amendments to other rules under the Advisers Act was borne out of the correct concerns to detect the indicators of fraud to help prevent it, to address the issues present in Long-Term Capital Management and to address the concern that its "current regulatory program for hedge fund advisers [was] inadequate".[41] A rule or rules to provide information with which to understand hedge funds and address these concerns was then, and is today, required, as long as it strives to avoid dual or duplicative regulation.

Goldstein involved a challenge to Rule 203(b)(3)-2 and amendments to other rules under the Advisers Act which removed the "look through" prohibition regarding corporate clients of hedge fund investment managers. Under Advisers Act s.203(b)(3), an investment manager that holds itself out as providing investment advice for compensation in a rolling 12 month period to 15 or more clients must register with the SEC under the Advisers Act. The SEC defined a "private fund" and, under Rule 203(b)(3)-2 and other amended Advisers Act rules, required any manager that advised a private fund to look through it and count the number of underlying clients towards the Advisers Act s.203(b)(3) 15 person threshold. The rule caught many managers, US and non-US alike, and resulted in an increased number of registrations. In striking Rule 203(b)(3)-2 and the other amended Advisers Act rules, the *Goldstein* court looked to the relationship between the manager and its "client" and held that it is the fund and not that entity's underlying investors that are "clients" and that the SEC's interpretation of the term "client" "falls outside the bounds of reasonableness".[42]

Certain persons may believe that *Goldstein* vacated both rule and rule-making (Release 2333 in its entirety). Others hold that *Goldstein* invalidated the new and amended rules but not the entire rule-making – those parts of Release 2333 directly implementing or interpreting Rule 203(b)(3)-2 and other amended Advisers Act rules would, by virtue of the rule no longer being in existence, fall away, while other interpretations and pronouncements, such as the discussion in footnote 201 of the definition of US persons, would survive. This writer believes that there is precedent for the latter position to prevail – but, if course, it is ultimately up to the SEC and the courts to ascertain which if these two results came about.

Goldstein did, however, refer to the SEC's position that the fiduciary duties that are created by the anti-fraud provisions of the Advisers Act reached the underlying investors of a fund[43] and confirmed that hedge fund investors "may sustain an action for fraud against the fund's adviser".[44] In this regard, the SEC has more than a legitimate basis to engage in a rule-making that would, within the parameters of *Goldstein* and *Fleschner*, protect the interests of investors in hedge funds from unscrupulous managers.

Valuations should be performed by administrators, independent of investment managers and prime brokers (and general partners), but with both of those parties given, after the calculations are made and the AUM and NAV per Share are published, all relevant information. Doing this would help realise the goal of ensuring a "robust independent valuation process" and prevent further instances of abuses such as in *Beacon Hill* and in Regents Park Capital Management LLP.[45]

Side letters, addressed in Chapter 5, are an issue for hedge funds from start up through year one, when large intakes are most needed. Side letters may, depending on the conditions that they require, be dealt with by making available to all investors the provisions sought by prospects, if possible, and by having clear Offering Material disclosure about the circumstances in which side letters should be given – and disclosed. If a hedge fund is listed, it may not be able to grant side letters on the basis that to do so would breach the listing authority's rules on equal treatment for shareholders.

Administrators are robust in checking investment objectives and policies, but must redouble efforts in monitoring investment restrictions, positions and position limits, and reporting their findings to directors and their fellow service providers on more than a quarterly basis (in conjunction with directors meetings). These reports should be provided monthly.

Whereas side letters and valuations have been "hot" regulatory topics, oversight is an issue that will attract scrutiny in the coming months. Historically, the hedge fund's promoter (investment manager or general partner) has played a "first among equals" role among hedge fund service providers. Investment managers (and general partners) have their own responsibilities *vis-à-vis* the hedge fund, but for them to handle the oversight role for the directors leads to conflicts of interest and the possibility that actions might be taken that, in certain jurisdiction, would lead to local tax authorities taking the position that an investment manager was taking decisions for the directors and taxing the hedge fund in that jurisdiction. The safe course of action is for the directors to exercise oversight themselves to ensure a proper relationship among service providers and correct reporting from them to the board – or, if sufficient funds are available, to employ a third party to perform this role. If it is ultimately decided that an investment manager would do this, proper resolutions need to be in place to authorise this and to ensure that the investment manager performs this role in accordance with proper conflict resolution procedures.

CONCLUSION

Countless books, articles, papers, conferences and journals have been devoted to hedge funds – to define them, shape them, discuss them and say what they do and not do. Others analyse the trading patterns of hedge funds. Countless others analyse risks, opportunities and rewards. This chapter and this book are not a definitive guide to hedge funds but do set forth current thinking about how hedge funds and prime brokers interact and relate to each other and how this relationship has changed since the first hedge fund took money and started to trade.

The remainder of this book flushes out prime brokerage, discusses service providers, analyses agreements and summarises tax, audit and accounting implications. Future editions will build on the premise of this book – which is that the hedge fund–prime broker relationship is dynamic, constantly being redefined and critical to our markets.

As we went to press,

The US hedge fund Amaranth Advisors LLC announced that it suffered trading losses of US$6 billion. The losses arose from trades in natural gas futures. It was reported that trades were placed on the assumption that the spreads between certain futures prices for natural gas would widen.[46] Instead, the spreads narrowed. The SEC, the FSA and other regulators are investigating the activities surrounding Amaranth's losses, as well as statements made by those connected to the hedge fund and/or others. It will take time to complete the investigations and to ascertain whether the trades that resulted in the losses were the result of a wrong call, risk management controls, missing important factors, unanticipated events or other factors – and to make changes, if they are required. While systemic damage may have been contained, the losses suffered by investors are large.

There are differences between Amaranth and Long-Term Capital Management. As pointed out in the Big Winners story, these included the amounts of leverage involved and the state of the debt and equity markets, and the fact that Long-Term Capital required a bailout of US$4 billion. There is also the matter of providing a remedy to those who suffered losses – and what those doing business with Amaranth may or may not have gained.

It was reported that Amaranth used "about eight prime brokers."[47] There are no indications whether having this many prime brokers was or was not a factor in the losses or the trading strategy: it may or may not have been. Certainly, each prime broker, as well as Amaranth itself, had and operated risk management tools. Judging by the facts that market participants, prime brokers and other players are sorting their positions and losses and that a central bailout does not appear to be required, Amaranth will not pose systemic risk.

Amaranth does, however, cast the spotlight on information sharing in the context of risk monitoring, given the numbers of those involved: several prime brokers, Amaranth's investment manager and others. Did the Amaranth losses occur because of a bad bet or a good bet that suffered from changed or unpredictable factors? Did one entity have information that, if shared, might have helped avoid the trading losses? Would more information or enhanced information sharing have resulted in the discovery of indicators or factors to have permitted Amaranth to adjust its trading strategy or to have minimized losses when the trades first "turned south"? It will be important to answer these queries to understand and sort out Amaranth, but also to help ensure that future situations are discovered before investors suffer losses and to protect our markets.

1 "Global hedge fund assets surge to US$1.5 trillion according to Hedge Fund Intelligence research", Hedge Fund Intelligence Press Release, 27 March 2006.

2 Feedback Statement 06/02, Hedge Funds: A discussion of risk and regulatory engagement, March 2006 available at http://www.fsa.gov.uk/pubs/discussion/fs06_02.pdf ("FSA feedback paper").

3 According to the US Securities and Exchange Commission, the first hedge fund was established by Alfred Winslow Holmes in 1949. *Implications of the Growth of Hedge Funds*, Staff Report to the US Securities and Exchange Commission, September 2003 ("SEC Hedge Fund Report"), at 3. See Hedge Funds, from Wikipedia, the free encyclopaedia, available at http://en.wikipedia.org/wiki/Hedge_fund

4 This discussion applies to an open-ended fund and not a closed-end fund. In this chapter, when we refer to a long only fund we mean an open-ended fund.

5 See eg, *The Challenges of Convergence*, Debevoise & Plimpton Private Equity Report, Vol 5, No 3, Spring 2005.

6 *See* "Management in an Era of Shareholder Activism", report by Morgan Joseph & Co., 31 July 2006 available from Morgan Joseph & Co.

7 *Soros Fund Makes Bid for Star Gas*, Gurufocus, 20 February 2006, available at www.gurofocus.com

8 *A Little Fund with Big Demands*, BusinessWeek Online, 23 May 2005, available at www.businessweek.com/managine

9 "Hedge Funds Hound Stork", Dealbook, 8 September 2006, available at www.dealbook. blogs.nytimes.com/?cat=22&nav=1

10 *Goldstein v SEC*, No 04-1434 (D.C. Cir. 23 June 2006) ("*Goldstein*"), at 2.

11 ("*IOSCO paper*"), available at http://www.iosco.org/library/pubdocs/pdf/ IOSCOPD213. pdf

12 Advisers Act Release 2333, 69 FR 72054 (10 December 2004) ("Release 2333").

13 SEC Hedge Fund Report at 3.

14 Hedge Funds and the FSA, Discussion Paper 16, August 2002 ("FSA Hedge Fund Discussion Paper").

15 "Testimony Concerning the Regulation of Hedge Funds", SEC Chairman Christopher Cox, 25 July 2006, available at http://www.sec.gov/news/testimony/2006/ts072506cc.htm

16 "Hedge Funds: An exploratory study of conduct-related issues", report by the Autoriteit Financiële Markten, 6 September 2005, available at http://www.afm.nl/consumer/default. ashx?DocumentId=5249

17 SEC Hedge Fund Report, p. 9, n. 27.

18 *SEC v Beacon Hill Asset Management, LLC et al*, Civil Action 02-8855(LAK) 15 June 2004 ("*Beacon Hill Amended Complaint*").

19 *Beacon Hill Amended Complaint*, at 38.

20 *Beacon Hill Amended Complaint*, at 40.

21 "Prospectus" refers to the document by which shares in a single entity hedge fund or in the "offshore feeder fund" in a master–feeder structure are sold, "Private Placement Memorandum" is the document by which membership interests ("Interests") are sold to US tax-paying investors in an "onshore feeder fund" and "Offering Materials" refers to both. In certain master–feeder structures, a single document is used to sell shares and/or Interests, and that document will be referred to as "Offering Materials".

22 Hedge funds should not select prime brokers solely on the basis of seed capital. Seed capital is one of several criteria that a hedge fund would use in selection a prime broker and it is

important to ensure that any commitment for seed capital is reduced to writing, disclosed in the offering materials, reviewed for legal, tax and regulatory implications. It is also critical to ensure that seed capital cannot be abruptly removed as this might cause precipitous drops in the NAV, kick off undesirable events, cause disruption to investing in the first, often the most critical year, and lead to redemptions from other investors. The letter memorialising the seed capital arrangement is a type of side letter, a topic that is discussed in Chapter 5.

23 As used in this book, "short selling" involves selling a security or other investment instrument and borrowing for delivery it in the hopes that the price of the borrowed investment will drop, permitting the seller to purchase that security from the market or another source and delivering it to the lender, making a profit on the differential. There is "naked" short selling, selling securities that are not owned, and "shorting against the box" (or "covered shorting"), which is selling short securities that the seller owns but, for various reasons, is not delivered.

24 "Alpha" refers to the difference between a return and a benchmark.

25 An absolute return fund is to be contrasted to a relative return fund, which measures the actual performance of the manager as opposed to performance against a market benchmark.

26 *See Moody's assigns first hedge fund operations quality rating* (5 September 2006), available at www.moodys.com/moodys/cust/research/MDCdocs

27 "Citigroup unveils new prime brokerage platform", MarketWatch Weekend Edition, Dow Jones, 2 August 2006, available at http://www.marketwatch.com/News/Story/9CrbKW296mFr9n8npZ5BxNg?siteid=mktw&dist=TNMostMailed

28 "The Need for Multi-Prime Brokers", Report by Paladyne Systems, LLC, 2 May 2006, available at http://www.paladynesys.com/NewsArticles/MultiPrime-Paladyne.pdf

29 According to *Capturing the sell-side upside*, IBM Business Consulting Services, 2004, citing Moskowitz, Eric and Katherine Burton, "Morgan Stanley Grip on Hedge Funds Slips, Bear Gains." *Bloomberg News.* February 9, 2004, "Goldman Sachs, Morgan Stanley and Bear Stearns share 'a combined 79 percent of the prime brokerage market'".

30 The Cayman Islands will begin to experience competition when Jersey and other offshore jurisdictions implement similar regimes and industry participants become comfortable with the single cell structure, implemented in Jersey and other jurisdictions.

31 S. 4(6) Mutual Funds Law (2003 Revision) of the Cayman Islands ("Cayman Mutual Funds Law").

32 ISE Listing Rules increase this figure to US$100,000 for funds that are not established in the EU, Isle of Man, Bermuda or Hong Kong.

33 S. 5(2) Caymans Mutual Funds Law.

34 ISE Listing Rule 3.A.1, amended by notice 12 April 2000.

35 An article in Bloomberg, "Hedge Funds Withdraw SEC Registrations After Court Rejects Rule" (22 September 2006), quotes the SEC as saying that 106 investment advisers deregistered after the *Goldstein* decision was handed down.

36 FSA Feedback Paper.

37 SEC Hedge Fund Report at 5.

38 SEC Hedge Fund Report at 4.

39 *Goldstein* at 4; SEC Hedge Fund Report at 46, 47.

40 SEC Hedge Fund Report at 4.

41 *Goldstein* at 7, citing Release 2333 at 72,059.

42 *Goldstein* at 13.

43 *Goldstein* at 15, n. 6. *See Abrahamson v Fleschner*, 568 F.2d 862 (2nd Cir. 1977) (*"Fleschner"*).

44 *Goldstein* at 15, n. 6 (citing *United States v Elliott*, 62 F.3d 1304, 1311–13, interpreting Advisers Act s.206).

45 FA Press Release, "Hedge fund manager withdraws from industry following fund overvaluation", 23 March 2006 (hedge fund manager overvalued portfolio).

46 Jenny Anderson, "Betting on the Weather and Taking an Ice-Cold Bath", The New York Times, 29 September 2006 ("Big Chill").

47 Big Winners.

2

Hedge Funds and Prime Brokers: The Legal Relationship from the US Perspective

Karrie H. McMillan, Larry E. Bergmann

Willkie Farr & Gallagher LLP

INTRODUCTION

The increase of active market participants in the 1970s created significant problems for the broker–dealer industry, which struggled with the massive amounts of paperwork required to clear and settle the transactions by these participants. As a result of this emerging problem, some brokers began offering what became referred to as "prime brokerage", designed to allow securities transactions executed at multiple broker–dealers to be cleared and settled in one account and at one broker–dealer. Although clearing and settling of trades remains a core component of any service package provided by a prime broker today, prime brokers now provide many additional services in response to the needs of growing numbers of sophisticated clients, in particular, margin lending and consolidated reporting to hedge fund managers. In addition to the increase in services provided by prime brokers, there has been substantial growth of the prime brokerage industry itself. In particular, the growth of hedge funds over the last two decades has led to similar growth in the prime brokerage industry. Prime brokerage was expected to generate revenues of nearly US$8 billion in 2006.[1]

This chapter will look not only at some of the more traditional services provided by prime brokers to clients that are hedge fund managers, but will also look at some of the more recent changes in the prime brokerage industry. The chapter will next discuss some of the regulatory issues that affect prime brokers and existing SEC and staff guidance with respect to those issues, as well as some recently settled enforcement actions involving prime brokers. Finally, the chapter will discuss some issues facing prime brokers going forward, including increased competition and some of the possible upcoming areas of regulatory focus of which prime brokers and hedge fund clients should be aware.

REGULATORY MATTERS

The prime brokerage industry in the US had its formal genesis in a no-action letter issued by the Division of Market Regulation of the SEC in 1994 ("1994 Letter").[2] This letter resulted from over four years of discussions involving the broker–dealer industry, represented by a Prime Broker Committee ("PBC"), and members of the staffs of the SEC, the Federal Reserve Board, and the New York Stock Exchange ("NYSE"). In the 1994 Letter, the SEC staff stated that it would not recommend that the SEC take enforcement action under certain US federal securities law provisions if broker–dealers provided certain services as contemplated by the terms of the 1994 Letter.[3] Absent the position taken by the SEC staff in the 1994 Letter, prime brokerage as we know it today would not exist.

The 1994 Letter described the prime broker relationship as follows:

❏ Prime brokerage is a system developed by full-service firms to facilitate the clearance and settlement of securities trades for substantial retail and institutional investors that are active market participants. Prime brokerage involves three distinct parties: the prime broker, the executing broker, and the customer. The prime broker is a registered broker–dealer that clears and finances the customer trades executed by one or more other registered broker–dealers ("executing broker") at the behest of the customer. Each of the executing brokers receives a letter from the prime broker agreeing to clear and carry each trade placed by the customer with the executing broker to whom the customer directs delivery of money or securities to be made to or by the prime broker.

❑ The customer maintains its funds and securities in an account with the prime broker. Orders placed with the executing broker are effected through an account with the executing broker in the name of the prime broker for the benefit of the customer. When a customer places a trade order ("trade date"), the executing broker buys or sells securities in accordance with the customer's instructions. On the trade date, the customer notifies the prime broker of the trade performed by the executing broker. The transaction is recorded in the customer's cash or margin account with the prime broker. At the same time, the prime broker records the transaction in a "fail-to-receive/deliver" account with the executing broker.

❑ The prime broker issues a confirmation or notification to the customer and computes all applicable credit and Regulation T amounts.[4] The executing broker confirms the transaction with the prime broker through the Depository Trust Company's Institutional Delivery System (today, Omgeo TradeSuite). The prime broker then will affirm the trade if its information matches successfully with the information received from the executing broker. The trade may then be submitted to the National Securities Clearing Corporation for clearance and settlement following normal settlement procedures. The prime broker then settles with the customer in the normal way.[5]

❑ The prime broker issues a statement of account to its customer on at least a monthly basis. The statement includes all security transactions during that period and the resultant customer security positions and money balances.

According to the 1994 Letter, the PBC believed that this arrangement benefited prime brokerage customers because the prime broker acts as a clearing facility and accountant for all of the customer's security transactions wherever executed, as well as a central custodian for the customer's securities and funds.

TRADITIONAL ROLE OF THE PRIME BROKER

Prime brokers provide numerous services to hedge fund clients, often providing a "one-stop shop" for many of the services that hedge funds need for their growth and operations. Traditionally, the primary services provided by a prime broker include:

❑ *Custody*: The prime broker safekeeps the fund's assets, reports on corporate actions of portfolio companies (eg, stock splits, dividends, mergers and acquisitions, rights issuances and spin offs) and provides other related custody functions. The prime broker also typically consolidates the custody of a hedge fund's various positions so that the fund can more efficiently use all of its assets as collateral for borrowing. Custody is of particular importance to hedge fund managers that are registered as investment advisers. Rule 206(4)-2[6] under the Advisers Act generally requires that a "qualified custodian" hold the assets of an adviser's clients. A qualified custodian under Rule 206(4)-2 includes broker–dealers registered under Section 15(b)(1)[7] of the Exchange Act. A qualified custodian also includes a foreign financial institution that customarily holds financial assets for its customers, provided that the foreign financial institution keeps the advisory clients' assets in customer accounts segregated from its proprietary assets.[8] While many hedge fund managers already had qualified custodians holding the assets of their hedge funds, this practice is now required for more hedge fund managers as more hedge fund managers have registered as investment advisers. In addition to safekeeping assets, many prime brokers will provide hedge fund managers with reports on corporate actions of portfolio companies and other functions related to custody.[9]

❑ *Settlement*: The prime broker has responsibility to settle trades placed by the hedge fund manager with the various executing brokers used by the manager.

❑ *Trade execution*: Prime brokers themselves will often execute many of the trades placed by a hedge fund manager (ie, the prime broker will also act as executing broker), although this may not be the case in the non-US models.

❑ *Reporting*: Prime brokers provide hedge fund managers with accounting and portfolio reporting, real-time portfolio tracking, on-line trade entry and other sophisticated reporting services specifically tailored to a fund manager's particular needs. The prime broker's reports may include daily profit and loss statements, valuation analyses, performance reports, position summaries, and income and expense summaries.[10]

❑ *Securities loans and borrowing*: Prime brokers provide securities for short sales. In connection with a hedge fund's short selling activity, the prime broker will locate the securities to borrow, clear the short sale, handle the collateral and margin for the fund, collect and pay interest on the short sale proceeds and calculate and pay any interest and any dividends due to the lender(s) of the securities.[11] When the lender recalls the securities borrowed by the hedge fund, the prime broker will typically try to find replacement securities so that the hedge fund does not have to cover the short position at that time.

❏ *Margin lending*: In addition to securities lending, prime brokers also provide financing for margin borrowing.[12] The prime broker's financing of margin is a critical source of liquidity for hedge fund managers that utilise leverage as part of their investment strategy. The revenue generated by prime brokers from securities lending and financing for margin borrowing is typically the largest source of revenue out of the various prime brokerage services provided to hedge funds.[13]

❏ *Access to securities offerings*: Prime brokers that are also investment banks can offer access to offerings of debt or equity securities. Offerings of new issues are subject to rules set out by the US industry's self-regulatory association, the National Association of Securities Dealers, Inc ("NASD"), including Rule 2790, which limits the ability of NASD members to sell offerings of new issues (ie, initial public distributions of equity securities) to certain persons, known as "restricted persons".[14] It is important for a hedge fund manager that wants its funds to participate in new issues to be familiar with applicable NASD rules, such as Rule 2790, because hedge fund managers will need to provide certifications regarding their status under Rule 2790 to prime brokers in order for a prime broker to be able to sell new issues to a fund. Prime brokers may also offer hedge fund clients access to private placements of debt or equity securities.

❏ *Capital introduction*: Prime brokers may also provide capital introduction services to hedge funds. This service, which may be of critical importance for fledgling hedge funds and their managers, can involve setting up meetings between the manager and potential investors, or more often, sponsoring conferences and seminars where managers and potential investors can meet. Prime brokers do not directly charge for capital introduction services, and do not receive fees if a potential investor places assets under management with a manager because prime brokers do not want their capital introduction services to be characterised as promotion of hedge funds, which would place additional requirements on the prime broker.

In addition to the services above, prime brokers may provide a variety of other services for new hedge funds, known as "incubation services". These services can include the provision of seed capital, office space, clerical support and other administrative services needed by the manager. Prime brokers often provide these services in exchange for the hedge fund generating certain amounts of revenue through trading, short selling, margin accounts and other transactions with the prime broker.[15] Hedge fund managers, however, must be aware of their fiduciary responsibility to get best execution for their clients and take that responsibility into account when selecting a prime broker. Managers should also be aware that many of these types of services fall outside of the safe harbour in Section 28(e) of the Exchange Act regarding the use of soft dollars.[16] A hedge fund manager that receives such incubation services also has an obligation to disclose that relationship to investors, particularly if compensation is paid to the prime broker directly, or in the form of brokerage commissions.[17]

Hedge fund managers, which typically have small staffs, need to have service providers that can address many of the middle office and back office responsibilities that the manager would otherwise have to handle internally. While many companies offer some of the services listed above, prime brokers provide a single source from which a hedge fund manager can receive all of the services.

PRIME BROKERAGE OUTSIDE THE US

As mentioned above, prime brokerage in the US is a creation of the 1994 Letter. US prime brokers must be sure that their agreements and the services provided under their agreements comply with the conditions in the 1994 Letter. For institutions outside the US, providing prime brokerage services to non-US hedge funds, the conditions in the 1994 Letter do not necessarily apply (unless the institution is subject to US regulations). Conditions such as a one-day limit for a prime broker to disaffirm a trade or label the trade as one the prime broker does not know ("DKs"), and minimum account capital requirements, eg, may or may not apply to the non-US prime broker, depending on local requirements and the PBA. Non-US prime brokers often provide substantially similar services to hedge fund clients as their US counterparts, however, the terms of the prime brokerage agreements will be driven by regulatory matters in the jurisdiction that governs the prime broker's activities, rather than the 1994 Letter.[18] Regulations will vary from jurisdiction to jurisdiction, and may be more or less comprehensive in certain jurisdictions. In a jurisdiction that does not have a regulatory regime governing prime brokerage, local contract law is likely to govern the terms of the agreement, and in those jurisdictions there may be more room for negotiating the terms of the prime brokerage relationship. Hedge funds seeking to enter into prime brokerage relationships outside the US should seek the advice of local counsel familiar with applicable regulations to assist in the negotiation of the prime brokerage agreement.

CHANGES IN THE INDUSTRY

The face of prime brokerage has changed significantly since the nascent stage described in the 1994 Letter. Traditionally, the industry has been dominated by three firms: Goldman Sachs Group, Inc, Morgan Stanley & Co, Incorporated and Bear Stearns Securities Corp.[19] While those three firms still hold a large sector of the industry, there has been an increase in competition from other firms, including UBS, Bank of America Securities, Citigroup, Lehman Brothers, CSFB and Deutsche Bank, among others. The increased competition, along with changing demands from clients, has led to prime brokers that offer additional and more specialised services than the prime brokerage services traditionally offered.

One such service is providing reports tailored to the needs of hedge fund investors. Institutional investors, such as pension plans, have placed significant amounts of money with hedge funds in an effort to diversify and improve returns; these investors, however, demand greater transparency from hedge funds in an effort to fulfil their own fiduciary obligations to their investors.[20] Prime brokers are in a good position to assist hedge fund managers in meeting these investors' informational requirements by packaging and delivering this information, such as fund holdings, to these investors. Receiving these reports from prime brokers, rather than from each hedge fund in which an institution invests, may provide greater consistency among the reports received, allowing for improved ease of review and analysis by their recipients. Prime brokers still need to rely on managers, however, for valuation methodology, particularly for illiquid or thinly traded securities.

Prime brokers are also updating their technology systems to provide better services to hedge funds and to differentiate themselves from others in the industry. Many prime brokers are developing "cross-margining" and "cross-netting" systems, eg, that allow them to calculate risk across a hedge fund's series of trades, rather than on a trade-by-trade basis.[21] These systems may allow hedge funds to maintain less cash or other collateral in their margin accounts at the prime broker because the combined risk across all of the hedge funds trades may be less than the risk of each trade on a standalone basis.[22] In addition to potentially allowing funds to maintain less cash in their margin accounts, the prime broker's calculation of risk across all of a hedge fund's trades provides a manager with an additional source of information to assess the overall risks involved with its trading strategy and can provide investors who receive risk-based data with a more accurate profile of the effects of the fund's strategies.[23]

One of the most significant changes has been a growing trend among hedge funds to use *multiple* prime brokers. According to research done by the Tabb Group, 56% of hedge funds managing more than US$1 billion in assets have more than four prime brokers, and 28% of such hedge funds use seven or more prime brokers.[24] Using multiple prime brokers has several advantages and disadvantages for a hedge fund. One advantage is that the increased competition can lead to better terms and rates for a fund. Another advantage is that prime brokers may have different expertise in locating different types of securities for short sales.[25] One broker may be better able to locate certain thinly traded debt securities, while another may have access to a larger pool of small cap equities for its lending programme. For hedge fund managers who prefer to execute trades primarily with their prime brokers, prime brokers will have different expertise in executing particular trading strategies. Maintaining several prime brokerage relationships may also give hedge fund managers, who are known for being highly secretive about proprietary trading strategies and portfolio holdings information, comfort that no single broker has records of all its investment positions and therefore would not be in a position to discern unique features of the manager's trading strategies.[26] Hedge funds managers using multiple prime brokers, however, lose the ability to obtain risk assessments and other analyses based upon the fund's entire portfolio and will not have the convenience of consolidated reporting. Their institutional investors that seek enhanced transparency also similarly lose these benefits, and may require more diligence of the manager, as risk assessments and other reports received from each prime broker will have data for only one aspect of the fund's holdings or strategies.[27]

THE LEGAL CONTEXT

The principal legal issue identified by the PBC in the 1994 Letter regarding prime brokerage arrangements was the application of Regulation T promulgated by the Board of Governors of the Federal Reserve System ("FRB").[28] The SEC staff noted that the arrangement additionally presented issues under credit regulation, customer confirmations, short sales, customer protection and net capital rules. Each of these matters is discussed below, followed by a summary of the staff's response.

Margin rule – Regulation T

Section 7 of the Exchange Act authorises the FRB to prescribe rules "for the purpose of preventing the excessive use of credit for the purchase and carrying of securities".[29] The extension of credit by broker–dealers to customers in connection with securities transactions is governed by Regulation T promulgated by the FRB.[30] Regulation T governs the purchase of securities by broker–dealer customers for cash, usually in a "cash account," or on credit in a "margin account". Regulation T sets the initial margin for a securities purchase at 50% of the purchase price (ie, the customer pays 50% of the purchase price and the broker–dealer extends a loan to the customer of the other 50%).[31] The PBC proposed that, for purposes of Regulation T, transactions effected for the customer, between the executing broker and the prime broker, should be deemed broker-to-broker transactions after completion of the affirmation process. The 1994 Letter described the operation of Regulation T to a prime brokerage agreement:

Regulation T requires a broker or dealer to record all transactions with a single person in a margin account unless specifically authorized for inclusion in another account.[32] ... Regulation T currently requires the executing broker to treat the customer as its own customer and record the transaction in a cash or margin account at that firm since it can be said that the executing broker is extending or arranging for the extension of credit to the customer until at least settlement date. The executing broker, however, generally settles prime brokerage transactions following normal settlement procedures through the prime broker's account at the executing broker, which is designated as a broker–dealer credit account. This method appears to regard the customer as an agent of the prime broker for purposes of these transactions, and to disregard the creditor/customer relationship between the executing broker and the customer.

Normally, under Regulation T, if a customer's margin purchase or short sale is involved, the executing broker would have to determine whether a margin deposit is required in a margin account.[33] The required margin amount would have to be deposited in the customer's account at the executing broker within seven [currently, five] business days after the margin deficiency had been created.[34] Regulation T, moreover, would require that the executing broker liquidate securities in a margin account to meet a margin call or to eliminate any margin deficiency exceeding US$500 [currently, US$1,000], if a margin call is not met in full within the required time.[35]

If the transactions were effected in a cash account, the executing broker would be able to buy from or sell to the customer a security only under certain restrictive credit conditions.[36] Transactions in the cash account are predicated on the broker accepting in good faith the customer's agreement that all securities sold have already been paid for and all securities bought will be paid for before being sold.[37] In this account, full cash payment for any customer purchases generally must be made within seven [currently, five] business days of trade date.[38]

If the customer has not paid in full for securities before the securities are delivered to the prime broker, the account at the executing broker would be subject to a 90-day freeze.[39]

The 1994 Letter noted, however, that in the prime brokerage arrangement, the customer never pays the executing broker, but rather the prime broker. Prime brokerage simply did not fit in any of the account structures of Regulation T. The executing broker–dealer had the principal relationship regarding transactions by the customer and therefore had the obligation to collect the Regulation T margin in the customer's margin account. However, in the prime brokerage arrangement, the prime broker maintains the customer's account and has the margin collection role. Although a broker–dealer could extend credit to another broker–dealer in relation to the other broker–dealer's customers' transactions, in a "broker–dealer credit account",[40] the prime brokerage arrangement involved the extension of credit by the prime broker to the executing broker's customer, not to the executing broker.

Issuing credit while part of a selling syndicate – Section 11(d)(1)

Section 11(d)(1) of the Exchange Act prohibits a person who is both a broker and a dealer from directly or indirectly extending, maintaining, or arranging for the extension or maintenance of credit on any security "which was part of a new issue in the distribution of which he participated as a member of a selling syndicate or group" within the prior 30 days.[41] Generally, this means that, absent an exemption, a broker–dealer customer may not purchase a new issue security from or through that broker–dealer on credit for 30 days after the completion of the broker–dealer's participation in the offering as a member of the selling syndicate or group.

Absent the prime broker relationship, Exchange Act Rule 11d1-1(a) permits the customer's purchase of a security from a selling group member to be financed in a margin account of a second broker (even one involved in the distribution) if the second broker did not arrange the transaction.[42] In a prime broker relationship in which the customer initiates the margin account with the prime broker, the customer generally can be viewed as having arranged for the credit provided through the margin account with the prime broker. Thus, when the prime broker is not a member of a selling group or syndicate, the prime broker's extension of credit for the purchase of the security through an executing broker that is a member of the syndicate is permissible as long as the credit extension was not arranged by the executing broker. Similarly, when the prime broker alone, or both the prime broker and the executing broker, are members of the selling group or syndicate, the extension of credit for the purchase of the security from the executing broker is permissible absent an arranging of the credit by either broker. Whether credit has been "arranged" by either broker is a question of fact that should be evaluated under the circumstances of each transaction.[43]

Issuance of securities confirmations – Rule 10b-10

Exchange Act Rule 10b-10 requires a broker or dealer, at or before the completion of a security transaction, to send its customer a confirmation of the trade.[44] The confirmation typically serves as an invoice and gives the customer an opportunity to verify and evaluate the details of the trade. The obligation to send the confirmation normally falls on the broker with whom the customer places the order because that broker generally has most of the information needed to comply with the disclosure requirements of the rule.

In the prime broker arrangement, the executing broker takes the order from the customer and issues a confirmation to the prime broker, but the prime broker typically issues the confirmation to the customer. The SEC staff noted that, while Rule 10b-10 required the executing broker to send to the customer a confirmation of each trade placed with the executing broker pursuant to the prime broker arrangement, customers generally do not want to receive individual confirmations directly from the executing broker, and would prefer to receive notification of transactions solely from the prime broker.[45]

Effecting short sales – Rule 10a-1

Rule 10a-1 under the Exchange Act prohibits any person, for his account or for the account of another, from effecting a short sale of a security covered by the rule under the following conditions: (a) at a price below the price at which the immediately preceding sale was effected ("minus tick"); or (b) at the last sale price if it was lower than the last preceding different price ("zero-minus tick").[46] The 1994 Letter also cited Rule 10a-1(c) as prohibiting broker–dealers from effecting a sell order without marking the order either "long" or "short," and noted that compliance with these requirements rested with the executing broker.

The 1994 Letter also stated that NYSE and NASD rules required the executing broker to ascertain that the shares will be available for borrowing in order to effect a timely delivery, and noted that the prime broker must also be aware of the nature of the sale because short sales must be recorded in a margin account and mar-gined in accordance with Regulation T.[47]

Net capital, reserve and custody requirements – Rules 15c3-1 and 15c3-3

Rule 15c3-1 under the Exchange Act sets out minimum net capital requirements for broker–dealers.[48] The applicable minimum net capital requirement for a broker–dealer is based on the type of business in which the broker is engaged and on the applicable ratio or minimum dollar amount set out in the Rule.

Rule 15c3-3 under the Exchange Act requires that a broker–dealer must promptly obtain and thereafter maintain physical possession or control of all fully-paid securities and excess margin securities carried by a broker for the account of customers.[49] Excess margin securities are those securities that have not been fully paid, have a market value in excess of 140% of the total debt balances of the cus-tomer's accounts, and which are identified by the broker as not being margin securities. Rule 15c3-3 also requires that broker–dealers establish a "Special Reserve Bank Account for the Exclusive Benefit of Customers." This reserve account must be separate from all other accounts of the broker–dealer and must maintain a minimum balance in accordance with the formula set out in Rule 15c3-3a.[50]

Although the 1994 Letter did not discuss the application of these provisions to prime brokerage arrangements, the no-action posi-tion incorporates terms reflecting these rules such that both the broker–dealers and the customers involved in prime brokerage arrangements must have significant financial resources.

The no-action position

The SEC staff, following consultations with the staff of the FRB, provided assurances that it would not recommend that the SEC take enforcement action if the executing broker and the prime broker treated prime brokerage customer accounts as if they were bro-ker–dealer credit accounts pursuant to Regulation T.[51] Transactions on behalf of the customer would be effected by the executing bro-ker and immediately sent to the prime broker. The prime broker enforces Regulation T *vis-à-vis* the customer (by collecting the required margin), and the broker–dealer credit account is used by the executing broker to record the transactions. By using the broker–dealer credit account, the executing broker did not have to collect margin in connection with the customer trades, and had fewer record-keeping requirements.[52]

The 1994 Letter, however, imposed 16 conditions on this relief that addressed Regulation T and the other Exchange Act provisions discussed above. Briefly, the conditions are:

❑ A broker–dealer must notify its self-regulatory organisation Designated Examining Authority ("DEA") that it intends to act as a prime broker.[53]

❑ A broker–dealer acting as a prime broker must have net capital of at least US$1,500,000.

❑ Broker–dealers acting as executing brokers that clear prime broker transactions or broker–dealers clearing prime broker transactions on behalf of executing brokers must have net capital of at least US$1,000,000.

❑ A prime broker may not settle prime broker trades on behalf of a customer unless the customer keeps a minimum net equity with the prime broker of at least US$500,000 in cash or securities with a ready market.[54] A prime broker also may settle prime broker trades on behalf of customer accounts managed by an investment adviser registered under Section 203 of the Advisers Act if each account has a minimum net equity of at least US$100,000 in cash or securities with a ready market.[55]

❑ Prior to the commencement of any prime brokerage activity, all parties to the arrangement must execute a contract that specifies their obligations and responsibilities regarding the prime broker arrangement. The prime broker and the executing broker must execute contracts with each customer on whose behalf the executing and the prime broker execute or settle prime brokerage transactions.[56]

❑ The prime broker must keep separate records identifying all customers using the prime broker arrangement, along with records of the executing brokers employed by such customers.

❑ For all transactions, by the morning of the next business day after trade date, the customer and the executing broker must inform the prime broker of the contract amount, the security involved, number of shares or number of units, and whether the transaction was a long or short sale or a purchase. Parties to a prime broker arrangement must utilise the facilities of a clearing agency registered under Section 17A of the Exchange Act for the issuance of trade confirmations and affirmations, and confirmations must be issued and received by the morning of the next business day after trade date.[57]

❑ The prime broker must be responsible for settling each of the customer's transactions placed with the executing broker and timely confirmed to and received by the prime broker in accordance with the provisions of item 7 above, unless the prime broker disaffirms or DKs a particular transaction by no later than the close of business of trade date plus one.[58]

❑ The prime broker must keep a record that identifies all trades disaffirmed during the previous three years, specifying the identities of the executing broker and the customer for each trade.

❑ The executing broker must comply with all the applicable short sale provisions and, prior to the execution of any short sale, the executing broker must determine that securities can be borrowed to deliver against the short sale.

❑ The executing broker may send the Rule 10b-10 confirmation to the customer in care of the prime broker if the customer has instructed the executing broker to do so in writing in an instrument separate from the prime broker agreement. On the day following the transaction, the prime broker must send to the customer a notification of each trade placed with the executing broker pursuant to the prime broker arrangement, based on information provided by the customer.

❑ The executing broker must keep and preserve the records required under Exchange Act Rule 17a-3[59] relating to trades placed with the executing broker pursuant to the prime broker arrangement.

❑ If the prime broker disaffirms a trade, the prime broker must send a cancellation notification to the customer to offset the notification sent on the day following trade date, and the executing broker must immediately send a new confirmation of the replacement transaction to the customer.

❑ If the executing broker was a member of a selling syndicate or group within the prior 30 days, the prime broker may extend credit on the offered security in a margin account previously established independently by the customer if this credit was not otherwise arranged by the executing broker, and a prime broker may extend credit in a prime broker account on a security sold by an executing broker if the prime broker has not otherwise arranged for that sale.

❏ The prime broker must treat the customer as its own customer for all purposes, including Regulation T and Rules 15c3-1, 15c3-3, 17a-3 and 17a-4 under the Exchange Act, if it does not disaffirm or DK the trade as provided above.

❏ Broker–dealers may not engage in prime brokerage activities with other broker–dealers or with customers if they know or have reason to know that such party is not in compliance with the provisions of the 1994 Letter.

In 1997, the staff of the SEC extended the no-action position taken in the 1994 Letter to prime brokers that have state registered investment advisers as customers, but that otherwise comply with the 1994 Letter.[60] This no-action position initially was temporary, but the staff made the position permanent in January of 2000.[61]

Section 206(3) of the Advisers Act and margin transactions

The SEC staff more recently addressed the application of Section 206(3) of the Advisers Act[62] to prime brokerage relationships in connection with questions concerning certain margin and short sale transactions. Section 206(3) states that it is unlawful for any investment adviser, directly or indirectly acting as principal for his or her own account, knowingly to sell any security to or purchase any security from a client, or acting as broker for a person other than such client, knowingly to effect any sale or purchase of any security for the account of such client, without disclosing to such client in writing before the completion of such transaction the capacity in which the adviser is acting and obtaining the consent of the client to such transaction. The section also provides that the prohibitions do not apply to any transaction with a customer of a broker or dealer if the broker or dealer is not acting as an investment adviser in relation to such transaction.

The SEC staff addressed a proposal by Goldman Sachs & Company ("Goldman"), which is registered with the SEC both as a broker–dealer and an investment adviser, by which it would provide margin credit to clients of Goldman Sachs Asset Management ("GSAM"), an affiliated registered investment adviser. [63] In granting margin credit, Goldman Sachs received a security interest in the securities, property, proceeds or other obligations that it held for a GSAM client. The staff took the position that the granting of a security interest for purposes of maintaining a margin account did not constitute a purchase or a sale of a security for purposes of Section 206(3), and therefore, the section was not applicable in this context. Goldman also had the right to liquidate securities to meet a margin call, if necessary. The staff took the position that in the case of liquidating securities to meet a margin call, Goldman was not acting as an investment adviser and, therefore, Section 206(3) also would not apply to that element of the proposal. With respect to short sales, Goldman requested that the staff take the position that the loan of securities to an executing broker to facilitate a short sale not be deemed an indirect sale of securities to the client. The staff agreed that the facilitation of short sales of securities by Goldman did not constitute a purchase or sale of a security from an advisory client, and that Goldman would not have to comply with Section 206(3).[64]

The present

The legal environment in which prime brokers must operate continues to evolve. As a consequence, the 1994 Letter is widely acknowledged to be in need of updating.[65] Some of the facts in the Letter have changed, eg, the Depository Trust Company has divested its confirmation and affirmation service, which services are now performed by Omgeo.[66] As indicated above, certain provisions of Regulation T have been amended.[67]

Most significantly, the SEC has adopted Regulation SHO, which introduced substantial changes to short sale regulation and affects the responsibilities of executing brokers.[68] For example, Rule 10a-1(c) cited in the 1994 Letter has been rescinded by the SEC and its provisions are now incorporated into Rule 200(g) of Regulation SHO.[69] In addition, Rule 203 of Regulation SHO, among other things, imposes requirements on executing broker–dealers to "locate" securities to borrow prior to effecting short sales.[70] In order to satisfy this locate obligation, the executing broker must either borrow or enter into a *bona fide* arrangement to borrow the security in order to make timely delivery on the short sale, or have reasonable grounds to believe that the security can be borrowed so that it can be delivered on the date delivery is due. In the prime brokerage context, the customer will often advise the executing broker that sufficient securities are available for borrowing from the customer's prime broker. Whether this representation from the customer satisfies the "reasonable grounds" requirement of Rule 203(b) is a facts and circumstances determination.[71] The NYSE has indicated that if a customer's prior assurance resulted in any *one* failure to deliver, the executing broker would not have reasonable grounds to continue to rely on that customer's assurances.[72] It is not clear, however, that the NYSE's position is required by the text of the rule or the SEC's guidance on the operation of Regulation SHO.[73] There seems to be an emerging expectation that in the prime broker context, the executing broker will need some level of information about the reliability of the customer's representations regarding the availability of securities to meet the locate require-ment, and that fulfilling this expectation will require communica-tion between the executing and prime broker about whether the securities "located" by the customer were delivered to the prime broker on a timely basis.[74]

The scope of prime broker/clearing broker liability for trans-actions effected by executing/introducing brokers is also under scrutiny.[75] In Man Financial, the NYSE found that the prime broker violated several rules, including the failure to have procedures to identify short sales in its prime broker customer accounts, as well as the failure to have procedures to make an affirmative determina-tion that securities were available or that Man Financial could bor-row securities on behalf of its client for delivery by the settlement date, prior to effecting a prime broker's short sale. In Bear Stearns, the SEC found that the prime broker, Bear Stearns Securities Corp. ("BSSC"), violated several securities laws by facilitating late trad-ing and market timing of mutual funds by clients of BSSC.

CHALLENGES FOR THE PRIME BROKER INDUSTRY
Areas of regulatory scrutiny
In addition to the recent regulatory actions brought against prime brokers, there are several additional areas that could become hot topics for regulators, such as capital introduction services, systemic

risk and money laundering. The prime broker industry has taken the view that capital introduction services are not "recommendations" of securities under applicable NASD rules because the prime broker typically does not have a customer-broker relationship with the investor and, therefore, NASD Rule 2310 regarding suitability is inapplicable.[76] Although many believe that this position is reasonable, the NASD has not provided formal guidance indicating its view on capital introduction services.[77] Also, although the industry takes the view that Rule 2310 does not apply to capital introduction services, it is considered a "best practice" in the industry for prime brokers to do some diligence on the potential investors to form a reasonable belief that the hedge funds are suitable. This reasonable suitability diligence is less rigorous than a full suitability analysis in accordance with Rule 2310. Many prime brokers conduct this diligence by checking to make sure the potential investors are accredited, have the potential investor fill out a questionnaire regarding their financial status and sophistication, and often impose a waiting period before inviting the potential investor to meet with hedge fund managers. This type of diligence is similar to the type of diligence discussed in the Lamp Technologies no-action letter.[78] Although the Lamp no-action letter dealt with the question of the use of websites in private placement transactions, the prime brokerage industry has used that framework as the basis for its practice in conducting basic due diligence. Many hedge fund managers that use capital introduction services from prime brokers will ask their broker to conduct diligence in a manner consistent with the Lamp Technologies letter. This diligence by the prime broker gives managers comfort that meeting prospective investors introduced by the prime broker is not likely to invalidate the private offering of their hedge funds or their exclusion from the definition of an investment company under the 1940 Act.[79]

Should the NASD conclude that capital introduction services rise to the level of recommending a security, then prime brokers would have to comply with NASD Rule 2310, which requires that an NASD member have reasonable grounds to believe that a recommendation is suitable for a client in light of the customer's stated financial situation, other security holdings, and needs. In addition to suitability questions, the SEC has inquired about potential conflicts of interest and disclosure obligations, for prime brokers and hedge fund managers, with respect to capital introduction services.

The SEC and its staff have expressed concern recently with the level of systemic risk that hedge funds pose, particularly in light of the growth in the number of these funds, the amount of assets they hold under management, and their use of leverage.[80] Prime brokers are some of the primary providers of financing that allow hedge funds to utilise leverage. Three particular concerns arise with respect to prime brokers financing the leverage used by hedge funds. First, some believe that prime brokers have loosened credit terms, allowing hedge funds to borrow more by committing less capital to secure their loans.[81] Second, the collateral used by hedge funds to borrow money may be illiquid and difficult to sell should the prime broker need to liquidate securities.[82] Finally, as hedge funds increasingly use multiple prime brokers, it is more difficult for each prime broker adequately to assess the risks associated with a fund's trading strategies and financial condition. The increase in trading of complex derivatives, which can be difficult to value and assign risk ratings, further raises the concerns associated with the use of multiple prime brokers and leverage by hedge funds. The risk is higher with respect to smaller prime brokers, who may be trying to gain market share by aggressively pricing their financing services, and which may not have the same level of oversight and risk management of the larger prime brokers.[83]

A third area of potential regulatory focus is AML. Registered broker–dealers, such as prime brokers, are required under the US Patriot Act and applicable regulations issued by the US Treasury Department ("Treasury") to have procedures reasonably designed to prevent money laundering.[84] Currently, unregistered pools such as hedge funds are not required to have AML procedures. The US Treasury issued a proposed rule in September 2002 that would require unregistered pools to develop AML procedures, but it has not yet issued final rules for those companies.[85] Likewise, the Treasury has proposed a rule that would require investment advisers to develop AML procedures,[86] but again has not yet issued a final rule. Many hedge funds and their managers have nevertheless adopted AML policies and procedures, in part because prime brokers typically require that hedge funds at least give representations or certifications regarding their AML policies in order for the prime brokers to comply with applicable regulations, which require that they have conducted reasonable diligence on their clients. In order for prime brokers to establish that they have reasonably designed AML policies, they may be required to show regulators that their hedge fund clients have conducted reasonable diligence on their investors, which could be difficult unless hedge funds do in fact have reasonably designed procedures and are willing to represent or certify to the prime broker that they have done such diligence.

Increased competition

Prime brokers are also facing increased competitive pressures, as many of the changes that have occurred in the industry are expected to continue. The lucrative nature of prime brokerage, and the continued growth of hedge funds, should bring new competitors, including service providers who previously operated in related, but distinct spaces, into the area that will place pressure on the ability of traditional providers of these services to retain market share.[87] As service providers attempt to create new products and services for clients, the roles of prime brokers, third-party administrators and technology providers are increasingly overlapping.[88] It remains to be seen whether hedge funds will be eager to further bundle services with one provider for the sake of convenience, or whether they will continue the trend of using multiple service providers. The answer will probably lie in the ability of individual service providers to offer expertise, superior service or lower rates to offset the convenience of having a bundled product from one service provider.

Hedge fund managers' use of multiple prime brokers appears likely to continue as well. In the world of registered investment companies (mutual funds or collective investment schemes), we have seen the trend towards the unbundling of services as funds and advisers seek out expertise in specific areas and realise that specialisation can outweigh the benefits of a bundled product. In the case of hedge funds and prime brokers, this seems especially relevant with respect to the ability of a prime broker to locate securities for short sales and the ability to service the increasing globalisation of hedge fund strategies. As hedge funds' trading strategies incorporate more complex derivatives and thinly traded or illiquid securities, the ability of a prime broker to locate those securities for short sales, as well as to help provide valuation and risk reporting with respect to those types of securities, will likely play a significant role in attracting and maintaining clients. The globalisation of hedge fund trading strategies places a premium on having a prime broker with good relationships and good contacts in whatever countries the manager is trading. The relationships not only help ensure that the hedge fund manager will have access to various executing brokers, but also help to ensure that it will be able to sell securities short and have a market to trade more illiquid securities in those markets. While the biggest prime brokers have a global reach, the ability of smaller prime brokers to gain expertise in specialised niches will likely attract some hedge fund managers.

CONCLUSION

The growth of the hedge fund industry has fuelled the growth of the prime brokerage industry as well. Prime brokerage, which began as a service to provide clearing and settling of trades, custody and reporting, has undergone significant changes with product and service innovation. Increasing complexity and the globalisation of hedge fund trading strategies, investments in illiquid or thinly traded securities and competition from new entrants into the field of prime brokerage will continue to bring changes to the roles prime brokers play with respect to hedge fund clients. As hedge funds and prime brokers try to keep pace with business changes, they must also remain aware that at least in the US, the eye of the regulator is for now firmly fixed on hedge funds. Scrutiny of these funds' primary service providers lies ahead, and likely will serve as a catalyst for future regulatory and business changes for the industry.

1 Serena Ng, "Moving the Market – Tracking the Numbers/Street Sleuth: Prime Brokers Get a Caution Flag – Credit Watchers are Wary of a Crisis From Lending For Hedge Funds' Trading", *Wall Street Journal*, March 8, 2006.

2 *Securities Industry Association Prime Broker Committee*, SEC No-Action Letter (January 25, 1994). Prime brokerage arrangements pre-dated the 1994 letter. *See, eg,* NYSE Information Memo 91-41 (October 18, 1991).

3 The 1994 Letter indicated that the staff's no-action position would remain in effect until December 31, 1995. Subsequent letters extended the position, and on December 30, 1997, the no-action position was made permanent.

4 Regulation T requires brokers and dealers to comply with certain conditions to maintain margin accounts for customers.

5 Typically, this involves crediting the customer's account with purchased securities and collecting payment, or crediting sales proceeds and withdrawing securities from the customer's account, on the third business day after the trade date. *Cf.* 17 C.F.R. § 240.15c6-1.

6 17 CFR § 275.206(4)-2.

7 15 USC § 78o(b)(1).

8 17 CFR § 275.206(4)-2(c)(3)(iv).

9 *See* "Hedge Funds and other private funds: Regulation and compliance", Gerald T. Lins, Thomas P. Lemke, *et al*, 2.3 (2005).

10 *Id.*

11 A US hedge fund recently filed a class action lawsuit in the US District Court for the Southern District of New York against multiple prime brokers alleging that the named prime brokers charged fees, commissions and/or interest as though the prime brokers had borrowed stock in connection with short sales by hedge funds and other prime brokerage clients, but the prime brokers failed to borrow and/or deliver stock in connection with those short sales.

12 Margin means borrowing money from a broker to engage in a securities transaction. The borrower must put up assets as collateral for the loan.

13 *Id.*

14 Restricted persons include other NASD members, personnel of broker–dealers and portfolio managers, such as hedge fund managers. Other than a *de minimis* exemption for accounts partially owned by restricted persons, NASD members are prohibited from selling new issues to restricted persons. The limitations on members selling new issues to restricted persons are designed to ensure the integrity of the public offering process through *bona fide* public offerings. Rule 2790 replaced the Free Riding and Withholding Interpretation, which limited the sale of "hot issues" to restricted persons.

15 *See,* Lemke & Lins at 2.3.

16 15 USC § 78bb(e).

17 *See,* SEC Hedge Fund Report at 84–85 (discussing SEC staff concerns regarding the provision of such incubation services).

18 Net capital of the prime broker, credit lending, custody and minimum account requirements are examples of issues that a non-US prime broker must address in light of the regulations applicable to the prime broker.

19 Serena Ng, "Tracking the numbers/street sleuth: hedge funds turn 'prime' brokerage into misnomer", *Wall Street Journal*, January 23, 2006 (available at http://www.post-gazette.com/pg/06023/643013).

20 Requests for more transparency have included requests for fund positions, risk assessments, disclosure of arrangements with service providers and the fees paid for those services. Investors generally have to request and often negotiate with hedge fund managers to obtain such information as managers are generally reluctant to provide information about their funds.

21 Tim Leemaster, "Banks vie for hedge fund cash", *The Standard* (July 11, 2005) (available at http://www.thestandard.com.hk/stdn/std/Markets/GG11Aug01.html).

22 *See,* the discussion of the concern of regulators regarding the systematic risks posed by prime brokers providing increased leverage to hedge funds.

23 *Id.*

24 Ng, "Tracking the Numbers/Street Sleuth: Hedge funds turn 'prime' brokerage into misnomer." *But see,* Paul Allen, "Prime time for primes", *Wall Street & Technology* (February 14, 2006) (stating that funds with US$2 billion to US$4 billion in assets under management are moving from having eight to ten prime brokers to two or three).

25 *See,* Ng, "Tracking the Numbers/Street Sleuth: Hedge funds turn 'prime' brokerage into misnomer."

26 Ng, "Tracking the Numbers/Street Sleuth: Hedge funds turn 'prime' brokerage into misnomer." We note that prime brokers should have compliance policies and procedures reasonably designed to ensure that the broker does not improperly use information obtained

from the hedge fund manager as a result of the prime brokerage relationship. *See, eg*, Section 15(f) of the 1934 Act, 15 USC 78m(f); Section 204A of the Advisers Act, 15 USC 80b-4a; NYSE Rules 92 and 342.

27 *See,* note 22.

28 12 CFR § 220.

29 15 USC 78g(a).

30 12 CFR § Part 220.

31 12 CFR § 220.12. After the initial purchase, the amount of margin required to be maintained is governed by SRO rules. *See, eg*, NYSE Rule 431.

32 12 CFR § 220.1(b)(1).

33 12 CFR §§ 220.4(b), (c) & .5(a), (b) & (c).

34 12 CFR § 220.4(c)(3).

35 12 CFR § 220.4(d).

36 *See,* 12 CFR § 220.8(a).

37 12 CFR § 220.8(a)(1) & (2).

38 12 CFR § 220.8(b)(1).

39 12 C.F.R. § 220.8(c).

40 *See* 12 CFR 220.7.

41 15 USC 78k(d)(1).

42 17 CFR 240.11d 1-1(a).

43 1994 Letter.

44 17 CFR § 240.10b-10.

45 *Id.*

46 17 CFR § 240.10a-1(a).

47 *See,* NYSE Memorandum 91-41 (October 18, 1991).

48 17 CFR § 240.15c3-1.

49 17 CFR § 240.15c3-3.

50 17 CFR § 240.15c3-3a.

51 The NYSE has adopted the provisions of the 1994 Letter for its members engaged in prime broker arrangements. *See, eg, Investec Ernst & Co*, Exchange Hearing Panel Decision 02-197 (October 2, 2002).

52 *See* "Securities Credit Transactions; Borrowing by Brokers and Dealers," 63 FR 2805, 2813 and n. 30 (January 16, 1998). In amendments to Regulation T adopted in 1998, the FRB explicitly recognised prime broker arrangements, and permitted prime broker transactions be processed in the "good faith account," 12 CFR § 220.6, rather than in the broker–dealer credit account, 12 CFR § 220.7. *Id.*

53 Section 17(d) of the 1934 Act, 15 USC 78q(d), provides that, where a broker–dealer is a member of more than one self-regulatory organisation ("SRO"), the SEC may approve arrangements for the SROs to allocate examination and other responsibilities among themselves. The SRO that is allocated with the examination responsibility is known as the Designated Examining Authority. *See* Exchange Act Rules 17d-1 and 17d-2 adopted under this provision, 17 CFR § 240.17d-1, 17d-2.

54 17 CFR § 240.15c3-1(c)(11) (defining the term "ready market"). The 1994 Letter also provided that prime broker transactions could be settled on behalf of customers that had at least US$100,000 in cash or securities with a ready market in its account if the account had a cross-guarantee of another prime broker customer that had a specified amount of net equity in its account with the prime broker.

55 *See infra* notes 61 and 62 and accompanying text for a discussion of this condition on state-registered advisers.

56 The Securities Industry Association has a form prime brokerage agreement along with other standard agreements available on their website at http://www.sia.com/standard_forms/.

57 At the time, this effectively referred to The Depository Trust Company ("DTC").

58 The ability of the prime broker to disaffirm trades was a significant and controversial element of the prime brokerage arrangement. The PBC had proposed that the prime broker have two business days to disaffirm a trade, but the SEC staff was unwilling to grant more than one day. The staff indicated that the ability to disaffirm is essentially inconsistent with the structure of a broker–dealer credit account under Regulation T.

59 17 CFR § 240.17a-3(a)(6), (7), (9).

60 *Ad Hoc Prime Brokerage Committee of the Securities Industry Association,* SEC No-Action Letter (July 9, 1997).

61 *New York Stock Exchange, Inc.,* SEC No-Action Letter (January 10, 2000).

62 15 USC 80b-6(3).

63 *Goldman Sachs & Company,* SEC No-Action Letter (February 22, 1999).

64 The staff did caution, however, that to the extent that GSAM recommends to a client that it engage in a short sale transaction from which Goldman Sachs might derive some benefit, GSAM may have a conflict of interest.

65 At the time of writing this chapter, discussions were taking place among members of the SEC, SRO, and industry staffs to update the 1994 Letter.

66 Securities Exchange Act Release No. 44189 (April 17, 2001), 66 FR 20502. *See* n. 57 *supra.*

67 In fact, Regulation T now explicitly recognises prime broker arrangements. *See* 12 CFR § 220.6(c); Securities Credit Transactions, Borrowing by Brokers and Dealers, 63 FR 2805, 2813 (January 16, 1998).

68 17 CFR § 242.200–203. *See,* Securities Exchange Act Release No. 50103 (July 28, 2004), 69 FR 48008 (adopting Regulation SHO).

69 17 CFR § 242.200(g).

70 17 CFR § 242.203(b). This provision supersedes former NYSE and NASD rules. *See, eg,* NYSE Information Memo 04-64 (December 22, 2004).

71 *See,* eg, Exchange Act Release 50103 (July 28, 2004), 69 FR 48008, 48014 n. 58; NYSE Information Memo 05-30, "The Exchange Publishes Lists of Pilot Securities Pursuant to Regulation SHO and Provides Guidance on the Regulation" (April 27, 2005), ("NYSE Memo 05-30").

72 NYSE Memo 05-30.

73 *See* "Division of Market Regulation: Responses to Frequently Asked Questions Concerning Regulation SHO," Questions 4.3 and 4.3(B), available at:
http://www.sec.gov/divisions/marketreg/mrfaqregsho1204.htm ("SHO FAQ").

74 *See* SHO FAQ Question 4.3(B).

75 *See, eg, Man Financial Inc,* NYSE Hearing Panel Decision 105–162 (December 22, 2005) ("Man Financial"); *see also, Bear Stearns & Co, Inc,* Securities Act Release No. 8668 (March 16, 2006) ("Bear Stearns").

76 Although the industry has taken the view that NASD Rule 2310 does not apply in the capital introduction context, the prime broker still has responsibility for the more basic suitability test; that there is a reasonable basis to believe the potential investments are suitable for the potential investor. This more general suitability analysis does not require a customer-broker relationship, which Rule 2310 does.

77 At least one commentator has taken the position that prime brokers who provide capital introduction services do need to comply with NASD Rule 2310 regarding suitability. *See,* Victor Zimmerman, Jr, "Hedge fund practices of brokers come under closer scrutiny", *Alternative Investment Quarterly* (Fourth Quarter 2003); *see also,* SEC Hedge Fund Report.

78 *See, Lamp Technologies, In.,* SEC No-Action Letter (May 29, 1997).

79 In particular, hedge funds that rely on the exclusion from the definition of an investment company found in Section 3(c)(7) of the Investment Company Act can gain comfort that the investors introduced by the prime broker are qualified purchasers as defined in Section 2(a)(51) of the Investment Company Act.

80 *See, Implications of the Growth of Hedge Funds,* at 1, 79.

81 Serena Ng "Moving the market – tracking the numbers/street sleuth: prime brokers get a caution flag – credit watchers are wary of a crisis from lending for hedge funds' trading," *Wall Street Journal*, March 8, 2006.

82 *Id.*

83 *Id.*

84 *Financial Crimes Enforcement Network; Anti-Money Laundering Programs for Financial Institutions,* 67 FR 21110 (April 29, 2002). *See also, Customer Identification Programs for Broker–Dealers*, 68 FR 25113 (May 9, 2003) (requiring broker–dealers to have customer identification programmes); *Financial Crimes Enforcement Network; Amendment to the Bank Secrecy Act Regulations – Requirement that Brokers or Dealers in Securities Report Suspicious Transactions* 67 Fed. Reg. 44048 (July 1, 2002) (requiring broker–dealers to file suspicious activity reports).

85 *Financial Crimes Enforcement Network; Anti-Money Laundering Programs for Unregistered Investment Companies,* 67 FR 60617 (September 26, 2002).

86 *Financial Crimes Enforcement Network; Anti-Money Laundering Programs for Unregistered Investment Companies,* 68 FR 23646 (May 5, 2003).

87 *See*, Tessa Oakley, "Custodian takes on frontline role", *Euromoney Institutional Investor* (August 1, 2002).

88 Paul Allen, "Hedge fund services heat up", *Wall Street & Technology*, February 27, 2005.

3

The Hedge Fund–Prime Broker Relationship from the Industry Perspective

Richard R. Lindsey

Bear Stearns Securities Corporation

With the growth of hedge funds over the last 20 years, there has been increased focus on the part of the securities industry that services hedge funds – prime brokers. Not only is this service function mostly unknown outside the hedge fund arena, many people who have spent their entire careers in the securities industry do not completely understand the role and function of the prime broker. This chapter provides a brief overview of the history, function and services of prime brokerage.

INTRODUCTION

At the most basic level, a prime broker clears and settles trades, custodies assets, lends securities and provides financing. The difference between a prime broker and what is conventionally thought of as a securities broker is that in prime brokerage, execution of the transaction may be handled by an entity other than the prime broker (or one of its affiliates). In large part, the prime broker performs for a hedge fund the role that a global custodian does for a traditional long-only mutual fund.

This is significantly different from how, for instance, a personal brokerage account operates. If an individual wants to trade securities, a broker–dealer is chosen and a brokerage account is opened. The broker provides that individual with execution, clearance and settlement, custody, securities lending, and financing. So why would a hedge fund want a prime broker? If an individual wanted to trade with (execute at) another broker, an account must be opened with that broker–dealer (which provides the same services as the first broker–dealer). In fact, if that individual wanted to trade with five different brokers, accounts would need to be opened with each of those broker–dealers. Further, if an individual wants financing of the positions at those brokers, the individual would be required to hold assets (or margin) in each of those accounts. The advantage of using a prime broker is that a hedge fund can hold all of its positions and the associated margin deposits in one account and trade at any executing broker.

It is generally accepted that the first hedge fund was a long-short equity fund created by Alfred Winslow Jones in 1949.[1] Jones can also be credited with the creation of the first prime broker: he hired Neuberger Berman to clear the trades for his fund while he traded at a variety of executing brokers. For several decades, this activity was known as "margin substitution" because it was an extension of the clearing function provided to specialists and floor brokers at exchanges (where the clearing firm substituted its strength and credit for that of the specialist or floor broker).[2] In 1983 Bear Stearns was the first major investment bank to offer margin substitution to "professional trading accounts"; thus it laid the groundwork for the development of the prime brokerage business as we know it today.

It was not until over a decade later, on 25th January, 1994, that prime brokerage was recognised by the regulators, when the Division of Market Regulation of the US Securities and Exchange Commission issued a no-action letter establishing a regulatory framework for prime brokerage.[3] The no-action letter was issued at the request of the Securities Industry Association's Prime Broker Committee.[4]

Today, there are about 30 prime brokers worldwide, with the top three firms – Bear Stearns, Goldman Sachs and Morgan Stanley – representing more than 60% of the market. Almost every hedge fund uses a prime broker in some way: to execute trades, to locate securities for borrowing, to provide margin financing, or to provide support for day-to-day operations. As hedge funds have grown in breadth and sophistication, the services provided by prime brokers have expanded. The role of the prime broker has

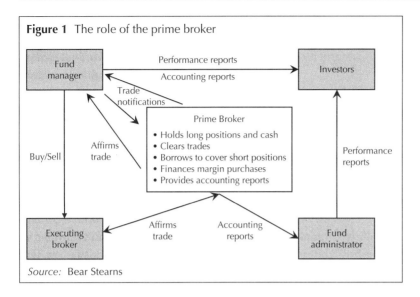

Figure 1 The role of the prime broker

Source: Bear Stearns

expanded from the basics of clearance, settlement and custody to the provision of products and services so hedge funds can focus on their core business of generating returns for their investors.

THE ROLE OF THE PRIME BROKER

Prime brokerage was traditionally viewed as a purely operational function responsible for clearing and settling trades, custody, and reporting of a hedge fund's trades (see Figure 1). Today, while prime brokers continue to offer those core services, they increasingly offer additional services including cash management, execution, office space, start-up services, capital introduction, consulting, and risk management services.

Core services

Clearance and settlement

The process begins when a hedge fund trades with an executing broker.[5] When the hedge fund enters into the trade, in addition to whatever the terms of the trade are (instrument, underlying, time, quantity, price, etc), the fund provides the executing broker with the prime broker's name and the relevant account with the prime broker.[6] This is known in the industry as a "give-up". The executing broker gives-up to the prime broker the trade, with the associated trade details. The hedge fund client also reports the trade (and any allocation of that trade) to the prime broker. If the trade details match, the prime broker confirms the trade with the executing broker and confirms the trade and allocations with the hedge fund. If the trade details do not match, the prime broker works with the hedge fund client and the executing broker to resolve the differences.[7]

In the give-up process, the prime broker may be acting either as principal or agent. When acting as principal, the prime broker is allowing the hedge fund to trade under the prime broker's name and is assuming the role of the hedge fund with respect to the executing broker, and the role of the executing broker with respect to the hedge fund, for all future cash flows associated with the trade. Principal prime brokerage is most common in the foreign exchange, OTC derivative and credit markets. Exchange or cash traded securities are usually cleared on an agency basis, ie, the prime broker clears and settles the trade on behalf of the hedge fund but does not assume counterparty risk.

Custody

The prime broker acts as the custodian, or, in Europe, sub-custodian, to hedge fund clients holding assets of the fund (cash, securities, contracts and claims) in accounts segregated from the accounts of the prime broker, its affiliates and its other customers.

Financing and margining

An important function of the prime broker is to provide financing to its hedge fund clients so they can obtain the leverage necessary for their strategies. Absent regulatory limitations, the prime broker determines the degree of leverage extended to hedge funds on a portfolio by portfolio (or client by client) basis, generally using a combination of stress-testing and value-at-risk. The leverage utilised by hedge funds varies widely, even within a given investment style. Table 1 is indicative of the leverage that hedge funds employ.

There are essentially two ways that a prime broker can extend leverage to a hedge fund client.[8] The first method is to provide margin financing. Under margin financing, the hedge fund borrows some portion of the security's value from the prime broker. By way of simple example, the hedge fund holds a stock with a value

Table 1 Representative hedge fund leverage

Strategy	No leverage (%)	Low (<2:1) (%)	High (≥2:1) (%)
Aggressive growth	20	60	20
Emerging markets	20	50	30
Equity market neutral	15	50	35
Event driven	15	60	25
Income	35	30	35
Macro	10	30	60
Market neutral arbitrage	10	25	65
Market timing	55	35	10
Multi-strategy	10	50	40
Opportunistic	10	60	30
Short selling	30	40	30
Value	20	60	20

Source: Van Hedge Fund Advisors

of €50 using €12.50 of the fund's assets and €37.50 of margin debt provided by the prime broker. As indicated above, margin debt is, in practice, provided on a portfolio of securities. So our example would be better stated as €100 million of positions, €25 million of equity and €75 million of margin debt for a leverage of 4 to 1 (assuming only long positions).

The second method of financing or extending leverage is through the use of derivatives, either in the form of OTC options or swaps.[9] While the structure of this form of financing varies, one approach takes the form of a managed account swap. In this case, the prime broker establishes an account advised (or managed) by the hedge fund manager who has trading discretion. The prime broker then enters into a total return swap with the hedge fund, and effectively transfers the economics of the account to the fund. The hedge fund manager trades the account to implement the hedge fund's strategy and receives, in the normal course, the returns associated with the account. The prime broker requires the hedge fund to post margin on the swap, and the amount of margin required determines the leverage used by the fund. So to follow the example above, the prime broker has an account with €100 million of its own assets. That account is advised by the hedge fund manager, where the hedge fund is the counterparty to a total return swap on that account. As margin for the swap, the prime broker requires the hedge fund to post €25 million of equity; thereby providing leverage of 4 to 1.[10]

In both cases the prime broker charges the hedge fund for the leverage that is employed. When margin debt is used, the prime broker simply charges the hedge fund interest on the debt. When a swap is used, the prime broker charges the interest in the form of a swap payment received from the hedge fund. The effective interest rate in both cases is generally the same since the two approaches are economically equivalent.[11]

Securities lending

Hedge funds sell short for a number of reasons: to implement long-short strategies; to speculate on "overpriced" securities; to implement merger-arbitrage and convertible arbitrage strategies; and as a hedge for derivative positions or restricted shares. Today, the daily total market value of securities lending (worldwide) is in the range of US$950 billion to US$1 trillion. For the hedge fund, the primary source of those securities is the prime broker.

In practice, the sourcing of securities for a loan actually starts with an investor agreeing to allow its securities to be lent. The investor may be a mutual fund, a pension plan, a custody bank or some other institution.[12] The securities are lent to the prime broker who provides collateral to the lender to secure the loan obligation. The current requirement is a collateral balance of 102% for US securities and 105% for international securities.[13] The prime broker then provides the security to the hedge fund, which sells the security short in the market. The proceeds from the short sale (the sale of the borrowed security) can be used to finance the purchase of other securities as long as the prime broker's margin requirements are satisfied by the portfolio of securities held in custody for the hedge fund.

An important part of the securities lending process is the manner in which fees or "rebates" work.[14] Consider, eg, a security lent by a custody bank. The bank, as agent for the investor, lends US$100 million of securities and receives cash collateral of US$102 million which the investor can either use in lieu of short-term funding sources or to invest in short-term instruments. If we assume that the bank invests the cash (for the benefit of the underlying investor) and receives LIBOR plus 20 basis points, the bank would typically rebate LIBOR flat to the prime broker, and keep 20 basis points of return on the cash collateral. In turn, the prime broker would typically rebate LIBOR minus 15 basis points to the hedge fund borrowing the securities, and keep 15 basis points of return for the cash collateral that the prime broker posted with the bank. The hedge fund therefore earns a "rebate" of LIBOR minus 15 basis points associated with shorting the securities.[15]

The example above is representative of the fee structure for what is known as "GC" or "general collateral", those securities which are in such plentiful supply in the market that there is a rebate associated with borrowing the securities. Securities where the demand for borrowing is quite high are known as "hard-to-borrow" (or "specials") securities and have a lower or even a "negative" rebate associated with their borrowing. In the case of negative rebates, the prime broker pays a fee (in addition to that earned on the cash collateral) to the lending institution and, in turn, charges a fee to the hedge fund. The size of the fee is driven by the market and varies from one hard-to-borrow security to another.[16]

Record keeping
As a regulated entity, the prime broker must maintain the books and records associated with each hedge fund account. These include all portfolio related information: trades and positions, interest and dividends, corporate actions, tax lots, position profit and loss and other account information.[17]

Reporting and statements
Associated with the record keeping performed by the prime broker is the production of reports and statements for the hedge fund. These include daily transaction reports, position level reports, cash balance reports, margin reports and other information associated with the activity of the hedge fund. These reports and statements are typically provided both electronically and on paper.

Ancillary services
Trade execution
While the ability to execute trades with a variety of counterparties is a key benefit associated with a hedge fund's use of a prime

broker, hedge funds often elect to execute some of their trades through the prime broker or one of the prime broker's affiliates.

IPO or issuance access

One of the primary reasons hedge funds use multiple prime brokers is to be able to access the flow of initial public offerings from those brokers. For those hedge fund with strategies which rely on the issuance of securities (eg, convertible arbitrage), this access is a key component of their relationship with a prime broker.

Research

Prime brokers may provide hedge fund clients with their proprietary research, access to management of corporations covered by their research analysts, third-party research, or incidental research such as economic or market information.

Technology

Prime brokers often provide a range of technology solutions to their hedge fund clients. Front-end trading systems are provided for order routeing and execution. Accounting, reporting and risk management systems are offered to assist hedge funds in their management of the business. Finally, most prime brokers provide systems or front-ends to ease the interaction with the prime broker and to deal with routine back-office activity such as wire transfers, corporate actions and trade reconciliation.

Capital introduction

Capital introduction is a commonly offered service by prime brokers. It consists of matching hedge funds and potential investors in those funds in a variety of forums. Generally, capital introduction is more of a "matchmaking" function where, eg, the prime broker arranges for a conference where a number of hedge funds are presented and investors attend to become acquainted with a broad spectrum of funds.

Consolidated reporting

In addition to the reporting of account information normally provided by a prime broker, some prime brokers provide consolidated reports of all trades or positions held by the prime broker and its affiliates. These reports consolidate positions across securities, foreign exchange positions, futures positions and derivative positions, and often consolidate the exposure to the same underlying security in a manner which makes it easier for the hedge fund to see its aggregate exposure regardless of the instrument.

Shadow reporting

Prime brokers may offer to their hedge fund clients the ability to consolidate the positions held by other prime brokers into one report. This is commonly called "shadow" reporting since those reports include positions that mirror or shadow the actual holdings at another prime broker.

Office space

Some prime brokers offer office space to hedge fund clients on a cost plus basis where the prime broker takes blocks of office space and sub-leases the space to hedge fund clients. This allows the hedge fund to obtain space at a lower cost (since the prime broker is using its purchasing power to negotiate for a larger quantity of space).

Start-up services

Many prime brokers provide special services to start-up hedge funds. Those services may include access to office space, assistance with technology and referrals to legal, accounting and administrator service providers.

Consulting services

Some prime brokers offer more generalized consulting services, much like start-up services, to their hedge fund clients. This consulting ranges from employment practices, recruiting, and human resources, to technology and hardware purchases and installation.

CONCLUSION

Prime brokerage is a relatively new business that developed in response to the growth of hedge funds over the past 20 years. It is an important service provided to hedge funds, and is constantly evolving and adapting to the needs of its clients. As hedge funds have become larger and more complex, prime brokers have expanded into more countries, markets, and instruments. For that reason, this summary of the role of the prime broker can only represent a snapshot of the business as it exists at the present time.

1 Jones operated an equity fund organised as a general partnership, which allowed it to hold both long and short positions and to use leverage. The fund was relatively unknown until *Fortune* published "The Jones Nobody Keeps Up With" by Carol Loomis in April, 1966.

2 For which, the clearing firm collected a fee and required margin or collateral from the specialist or floor broker. In exchange, the clearing firm substituted its margin or collateral for that of the smaller, less well capitalised specialist or floor broker with the counterparty – or, from another angle, the specialist "substituted" its counterparty margin requirement with margin by its carrying broker.

3 http://www.sec.gov/divisions/marketreg/mr-noaction/pbroker012594-out.pdf. The original no-action letter was made permanent by a subsequent letter dated 30th December, 1999. *See* http://www.sec.gov/divisions/marketreg/mr-noaction/nyse123099a-out.pdf

4 The request is in two letters, dated 13th September, 1989, and a follow-up dated 3rd June, 1991, both addressed to the Board of Governors of the Federal Reserve System.

5 While the executing broker could be the prime broker or one of its affiliates, it is assumed here that it is an unaffiliated broker. In any event, the process is nearly identical.

6 When a hedge fund opens an account at a prime broker, notification is sent using a Form 1, Schedule A to all of the intended executing brokers of the fact that trades can be given up to that prime broker.

7 This is a simplified version of the process. For exchange traded securities where there is a clearing house involved as the central clearing counterparty, an affirmation and confirmation procedure may be used.

8 A third method, used for primarily for government securities, is the use of repo financing.

9 Such approaches are often referred to as synthetic prime brokerage.

10 In the cases of both the swap and the margin loan, the positions are marked to market daily.

11 While the two methods of financing are economically equivalent, they are not legally equivalent. Margin debt is extended under an institutional account agreement which gives the prime broker a perfected security interest in the securities held in the portfolio. Swaps or OTC derivatives are subject to ISDA agreements which have different terms from an institutional account agreement, and the portfolio actually belongs to the prime broker.

12 For a custody bank to lend the securities that it holds in custody there must be a lending agreement with the beneficial owner of those securities. In addition, the investor could be an individual or any security holder. Normally a security that is margined can be rehypothecated by the margin lender. Margin accounts at a broker–dealer may therefore be a source of securities for lending.

13 The collateral requirement is generally satisfied with cash or near-cash instruments and is marked to market daily.

14 In the US, charges for securities lending are quoted as rebates; in Europe, as fees.

15 Securities lending is often an inexpensive form of financing for some institutions or, alternatively, a method of obtaining additional return on a portfolio of securities. For example, in its 2005 annual report, the Harvard Endowment indicates that, as of 30th June, 2004, the endowment had generated more than US$5.8 billion of cash flow from its securities lending activity (http://vpf-web.harvard.edu/annualfinancial/pdfs/2005statements.pdf).

16 In recent years, for some very hard-to-borrow securities, negative rebates have reached as high as 20% (annualized); in other words, a hedge fund pays 20% per year to hold the short position on the security.

17 A prime broker only knows the information associated with those trades that the hedge fund chooses to custody with that prime broker. In general, the prime broker will not know positions held at other prime brokers, at banks, physical assets, or off-balance sheet positions.

REFERENCES

Hintz, B., T. Buechs, and M. I. Levy, 2005, *US Securities Industry: The Power of Prime Brokerage*, Bernstein Research Call, February 24.

Investors Services Journal, 2005, *Securities Lending Market Guide*.

Lee, S., 2002, *Prime Brokerage: One Service to Bind Them All*, Celent Communications, February.

Rich, D. and J. A. Moore, 2002, "Scope and Dynamics of the Securities Lending Industry", *The Journal of Portfolio Management*, **29(1)**, pp 61–75.

Tiernan, L. and A. Bates, 2000, *Irish Domiciled Hedge Funds and the Role of the Prime Broker*, Dillion Eustace.

Valentine, D., 2004, *The Burgeoning Business of Prime Brokerage*, Celent Communications.

4

"Related Parties" and their Role in the Relationship

Bruce Gardner

SJ Berwin LLP

INTRODUCTION

Hedge funds take various forms. Due to most hedge fund strategies involving trading activity (generating income) as opposed to investment activity (generating capital return), the majority of European-managed hedge funds are structured as corporate vehicles incorporated in one of the tax haven jurisdictions, typically the Cayman Islands. A corporate vehicle is opaque in the sense that the vehicle itself carries on the trading activity of the fund rather than the returns flowing directly through to investors as in a transparent partnership structure. However, in the case of US-domiciled funds and offshore funds structured for US tax-paying investors, the structure will often take the form of a transparent limited partnership whose general partner is primarily responsible for the management of the overall affairs of the fund and acts as investment manager. Whichever structure is adopted, one common feature is that neither the board of the corporate hedge fund nor the board of the general partner in a limited partnership structure participates in the day-to-day management, operation and administration of the fund. These three critical functions are effectively delegated and divided between the manager, the prime broker and the administrator who must work effectively with the board and with each other so as to ensure that the fund can operate effectively, make money and protect investors' interests are protected.

Although the principal trading and administration functions are delegated by the board, the directors of the fund remain ultimately responsible for the creation of this network of service providers, for the selection and supervision of the providers themselves and for the review and approval of the documentation appointing them. A typical split of functions would involve the fund's investments being managed by the manager, its books of account and investor records being maintained by the administrator, who will also carry out the critical function of valuation of the fund's assets and production of the "NAV" calculations and the prime broker who is appointed to execute and/or clear and settle trades, acts as custodian and act as the provider to the fund of stock loans, financing and leverage. In certain jurisdictions, the fund will also be required to have a custodian to hold the assets.

There are generally regarded to be three critical relationships within the overall hedge fund structure, namely the relationships between: the fund's board and the prime broker; the fund's board and the administrator; and the board and the prime broker. Each of these three must, however, also interact with the fund's manager. The roles of risk managers, regulators and custodians are all also crucial to the efficient operation of the fund. This chapter will consider the relationship between the hedge fund and the following entities:

❏ the board of directors;
❏ the manager;
❏ the administrator;
❏ the executing broker;
❏ the custodian or sub-custodian;
❏ the risk manager;
❏ the exchanges; and
❏ the relevant regulator.

The chapter will also consider the relationships and legal implications of the interactions between the service providers themselves. Certain requirements of a regulatory nature, such as AML and "know your client" requirements, which are summarised separately in this chapter, impact upon all service providers in the matrix to varying degrees, and the changing regulatory framework and its impact on the various players is also assessed.

THE RELATIONSHIP BETWEEN THE PRIME BROKER AND THE BOARD OF DIRECTORS

As stated previously, the board of the fund retains ultimate responsibility for the appointment and supervision of the prime broker, as well as the other service providers. In instances of default of the fund, it could be open to investors to change the board of directors, appoint a liquidator and take action against directors in certain circumstances, and directors clearly need to take their responsibilities seriously in this regard.

Directors of hedge funds can either be "interested" or "independent". Interested directors are employees of the fund's manager, whilst independent directors do not have any significant relationship with the fund's manager and, arguably, its other service providers. Independence of directors has become an important consideration not only for those funds that seek a listing on a stock exchange,[1] but also from the perspective of investors' expectations. Whatever the status of the directors, however, the board should have sufficient collective expertise to be able to understand the fund's trading and the nature of its underlying investments, including its risk-profile and liquidity. The board should also be able to evaluate the fund's performance, and have in place a structure which allows regular review of the service providers to ensure that they continue to provide a competitive and effective service to the fund. In practice, the board would rely on the manager to assist with this process as long as relevant tax and corporate governance requirements are observed.

Fundamentally, it is crucial that the fund and its directors are satisfied that the prime broker is financially secure, well capitalised and has an acceptable credit rating, where applicable. The board should also consider the adequacy of the prime broker's risk management and control. If the prime broker is not managing and controlling its risk on a real-time basis, the fund could be exposing itself to the risks arising from overtrading by another prime broker's client. In addition, the board should consider how the fund's assets in custody with the prime broker but not used as collateral or for margin purposes are held, and whether these assets are vulnerable to third party credit risk.

To this end, it is worth noting that under the Capital Requirements Directive, which will come into force on 1 January 2007, a prime broker regulated in the UK will be required to have a contingency and business continuity plan in place to ensure its ability to operate on an ongoing basis and to limit losses in the event of severe business disruption. The prime broker will be required to establish, implement and maintain an adequate business continuity policy aimed at ensuring that its essential data and functions are preserved, and its investment services and activities maintained in the case of an interruption to its systems and procedures. Where that is not possible, a firm will need to enable the timely recovery or resumption of such data, functions, services and activities.[2] This policy provides an added protection to the fund in case of a significant disruption to business, such as an act of terrorism. Moreover, the FSA's expressed interest in the prime broker's prudential stability, discussed below, is also of note.

Prior to appointing the prime broker and approving any relevant documentation, the directors may wish to pay particular attention to the following common issues, although, these are by no means exhaustive:

❏ Definition of services
❏ Fees
❏ Events of default and close-outs
❏ Collateral and security
❏ Appointment of sub-custodians
❏ Treatment of cash
❏ Confidentiality
❏ Choice of law and disputes.

Definition of services
As discussed in other chapters, notably Chapter 5, in addition to providing clearing and settlement facilities and reporting of the fund's trades, prime brokers provide cash and securities loans, thereby facilitating short sales and on-margin purchase of securities. Prime brokers also provide custodial services, but usually only in order to secure and facilitate the margin lending activities and the associated collateral movements. Some funds, such as those with a trading strategy of buying and selling exchange-traded derivatives,

will not need the services of a prime broker at all, whilst some funds that require greater leverage or take large short positions may have more than one prime broker. Whatever the particular characteristics of the strategy, however, it is important that the services to be provided and the standards to be observed are sufficiently well specified to ensure that the fund is justified in entrusting its operations to the prime broker.

Fees

A number of fees will be payable to the prime broker for the services provided to the fund. The fees include execution fees, clearing and settlement fees, stock-lending fees if the fund wishes to take short positions, margin-lending fees, haircuts on repos and various other fees if engaging in derivatives transactions. As discussed later in this chapter, the fund may chose different executing brokers who offer cheaper execution services, however, the fund usually does not have a choice of providers for the other mentioned services. The directors should have an understanding of the fee structure and its financial implications for the fund.

Events of default and close-out

The Prime Brokerage Agreement is likely to specify a series of "events of default", and the directors will want to ensure that these are as reasonable and narrow as possible so that the prime broker is not given power to enforce against the fund other than in wholly appropriate circumstances or to even "control" the fund. One school of thought is that the prime broker is likely to exercise extreme caution before choosing to default the fund and close-out in view of the significant implications this may have including, in extremist, the demise of the fund. On the other hand, if the default or anticipated default arises as a result of some weakness or feature of the trading strategy employed by the fund where the prime broker provides similar services to other funds with the same strategy it may be effectively forced to default the fund (and others) in order to avoid unacceptable aggregated exposure. This is a difficult balancing act, and may also be affected by the increasingly close prudential relationship between prime brokers and regulatory authorities, discussed in the paragraph overleaf and the need to control systemic risk.

Where there are multiple agreements in place between the fund and the prime broker, in the event of default on one agreement, the prime broker may be entitled to close out the fund's positions under any of the applicable agreements. The directors should, therefore be aware of the cross-default provisions in the prime brokerage documents.

The directors should also be aware that in the event of default by the fund, it would be the prime broker who performs the calculation of the close-out amount or default market value for the purposes of set-off and netting arrangements and settlement amounts due.

Collateral and security

In stock-lending and equivalent types of transactions the directors need to understood how this is undertaken, and ensure that the documentation which empowers the prime broker also requires it to protect the interests of the fund by, ensuring timely provision of collateral marked-to-market.

Most funds are dependent on their prime broker, who usually holds all of the fund's assets in custody in order to facilitate timely cash and stock lending. This exposes the fund and its shareholders to additional risks. In the event of a default by the fund, the prime broker can recover the amount owing through sale of the fund's assets, however, in the event of insolvency by the prime broker the fund may not be able to recover some or all of its assets (cherry-picking in the absence of effective netting and set-off arrangements).

In addition, it is important to bear in mind that the assets of the fund held by the prime broker can often be rehypothecated and may be subject to onward dealing. Therefore, securities could be taken out of the fund's assets at any time pursuant to a repo/stock lending transaction between the prime broker and a third party, and replaced by the prime broker with equivalent securities or under certain circumstances, cash.

Appointment of sub-custodians

With respect to custody arrangements, the directors need to understand and consider the manner in which the prime broker will perform or sub-delegate the performance of custody. The conventional standard of care for the custodian in selection of sub-custodians in different jurisdictions is that the custodian takes responsibility for those sub-custodians that are its associated entities, but in relation to selection of true third-party entities the custodian's duty is to select and retain them with prudence, but not (usually) to be liable for losses beyond this.[3]

In like manner to a prime broker holding custody of the fund's assets, the sub-custodian may also be able to rehypothecate the assets of the fund and make them subject to onward dealing if so provided in the Prime Brokerage Agreement. This is of particular significance to the directors in instances where the sub-custodians are third parties not affiliated with the prime broker, as it may be difficult for the fund to ensure that its assets are properly accounted for and adequately replaced, or to recover its assets in case of insolvency of the sub-custodian.

Treatment of cash

The directors should be aware that the PBA often specifies that the money received from the fund and held by the prime broker on the fund's behalf, is not treated as client money and as such not subject to the protections conferred by the FSA Client Money rules in the Client Assets Sourcebook. Consequently, in the event of insolvency by the prime broker the fund would not have immediate access to its money in the prime broker's account, but would be considered as an unsecured creditor.

Indemnity

Directors should be aware that the fund will undoubtedly be required to indemnify the prime broker against any loss, damage, cost or expense related to the transactions and relationship established by the Prime Brokerage Agreement. In certain cases, the fund may be asked to agree to cover the reasonable costs, expenses and legal fees of counsel chosen by the prime broker. Clearly, this is a potentially substantial exposure and the directors should be aware of, and where possible limit the liability and the indemnity.

Confidentiality

Due to the nature of their relationship, the prime broker has knowledge of the fund's positions and investment strategies, all of which is commercially sensitive information. The directors should ensure that all information and advice the fund, through the manager and its administrator, provided to the prime broker is treated as confidential and not disclosed to third parties without the fund's prior written consent. It should be borne in mind that the confidentiality is inevitably restricted to the extent that the prime broker may make any disclosure required by law or applicable regulations. As discussed below, the FSA is increasingly relying on the prime brokers to disclose information about hedge funds, both for the purpose of general information gathering and in enforcement investigations.

Choice of law

If both the prime broker and the fund are located in the same jurisdiction, and the contract is silent on the choice of law and forum, generally speaking the law of the place where the contract was made will be applied to the interpretation of the contracts and in litigation. However, as it is likely that the fund and the prime broker will not be domiciled in the same jurisdiction, and that the commercial activity will not be limited to their domicile jurisdictions, the directors will need to understand which law is to be applied in the event of a dispute. The parties to a contract are free to make a choice of law and choice of forum, even if there is no other connection between the substance of the obligations and the law selected. The choice of law is particularly important in instances where a decision would be different depending on which law the court applies.

The prime broker is likely to choose the law of its own domicile and may seek exclusive jurisdiction in litigation for the courts of that domicile. In practice the directors may not hold a strong bargaining position, however, in order to avoid potential problems associated with exclusive jurisdiction, it would be advisable to always seek selection of non-exclusive jurisdiction.

AML and know your client ("KYC") obligations

With regard to the impact of AML and KYC requirements, these tend to be delegated to the administrator (even if the administrator is domiciled in a different jurisdiction), rather than being the primary responsibility of the board or the prime broker, however, Cayman funds are themselves subject to Cayman Islands AML provisions. Accordingly, if the directors of a Cayman fund, (or any person for that matter) suspects that a payment to the fund whether by way of subscription or otherwise, is the proceeds of crime, they are required to make a report to the relevant authorities. Directors also have the power to withhold the payment of redemption in such circumstances. The withheld redemption payment should be deposited with the custodian until such time as the payment to the investor or shareholder is approved by the directors.

Similarly, the prime broker will itself be subject to AML obligations and should be aware of such requirements as its services the day to day trading activities of the fund.

THE FUND MANAGER

Whilst the funds are lightly regulated and are typically domiciled offshore, the FSA and other regulators authorise and regulates the managers and their activity in the UK. In the US since February 2006, managers were required to be registered with the SEC: this requirement was overturned in *Goldstein*.[4] The current regulatory trends are discussed below.

The manager's relationship with the fund is governed by the terms of the Investment Management Agreement. The manager advises the fund and constructs the funds' investment and trading strategies. The manager's who in essence facilitates the effective implementation of the fund's investment objectives and policies strategy, determines the success of the strategy and in turn of the performance of the fund.

The Prime Brokerage Agreement recognises that the fund delegates its trading authority to a manager and requires that the prime broker is notified in writing of this delegation, including sight of a trading authorisation or a copy of the Investment Management Agreement. The fund also needs to authorise the prime broker to act on the proper instructions of the manager, so that any such instructions may be deemed as instructions from the fund itself. In the event that the fund modifies, limits or cancels the trading authority granted to the manager, the prime broker should be notified at the earliest opportunity. The Prime Brokerage

Agreement also needs to address any specific jurisdictional restrictions, such as instructions being limited to execution, clearing, settlement and custody of trades or positions of non-US securities. The fund would ordinarily indemnify the prime broker against any losses incurred as a result of or in connection with the proper performance of the prime broker's obligations pursuant to instructions received from the manager.

What must the manager look for in the prime broker?

The fund appoints the prime broker, the manager advises the fund in this process. When advising on the appointment of the prime broker, the manager should consider and advise the fund's directors on the following matters:

(a) Can the prime broker provide the sort of service that both the fund and manager require, so that the fund's trading strategy is effectively implemented?

(b) Does the prime broker in practice understand the trading strategy?

(c) Is one prime broker sufficient or should there be two or more?

(d) How are issues such as custody and stock-lending dealt with in the PBA, and is there evidence from the information available to the manager that establishes how these issues will be dealt with in practice?

(e) Last, but certainly not least, does the service represent value for money to the fund, taking into consideration all sorts of issues ranging from the manager's bargaining position to the prime broker's capacity to save cost through aggregation of services?[5]

The selection of a well-respected and qualified prime broker is likely to maintain investor confidence.

Facilitation of trades and investment strategies

The prime broker controls the trading of the fund, in effect, through the provision of the key functions of clearing of the fund's investment trades, but also through the provision of cash and stock-lending facilities. The quality of a prime broker's stock-lending capability is arguably the most crucial factor in the success of a manager whose strategy involves short selling. Some prime brokers might have exclusive sources of supply, which give the manager the ability to access "hard to borrow" stocks at competitive rates.

It is through the prime broker's financing across a range of assets, that the manager achieves the required leverage in trading. This is important, especially for managers engaging in market neutral trades and building performance on small profit margins for each trade. The prime broker can calculate the amount of leverage available using either a simple rules-based process, such as a percentage of individual positions or combined strategies, or a more complex value-at-risk (VAR) model, which aims to measure the risk of a portfolio at any given time. Development of VAR margin lending has led to more aggressive financing and higher leverage.

Another important facility for a fund manager, which a prime broker can provide though its economies of scale, is to allow the manager to leverage off the prime broker's balance sheet strength, and thereby gain access to trades that might otherwise be inaccessible on an individual fund basis.

Best execution

The manager should have efficient data exchange with the prime broker, and should be provided with an integrated desktop solution to facilitate the timely feeding of information.

The manager is obliged to provide to the fund "best execution", an obligation which the manager cannot renounce just because it is conducting its trading through the prime broker. In the UK, the prime broker too is obliged to provide "best execution" to the manager, unless the manager as an intermediate client has waived that right. Currently, as an intermediate customer, the fund can opt out of this entitlement. It should be noted, however, that under the Market in Financial Instruments Directive, (in force from 1 November, 2007 ("MIFID")), the manager under the new category of a professional client will no longer be able to waive its right to best execution. This means that both the manager and the prime broker will have to have in place, and continuously monitor, policies that adequately address how best execution is to be provided, taking into account the fund's trading strategy, and the relative liquidity of the desired stock.

AML and KYC obligations

Again, while funds delegate the performance of various AML and KYC requirements to the administrator where possible, certain AML and KYC obligations are imposed on both the manager and the prime broker if authorised in the UK. These requirements are set out in the some detail below.

THE ADMINISTRATOR

In order to understand the relationship between the prime broker and the administrator, one must have a clearer understanding of the of administrator's (ever expanding) functions.

The Administration Agreement sets out the relationship between the fund and the administrator. This agreement sets out in detail the duties to be undertaken by the administrator in its capacity as administrator of the fund. The Administration Agreement is sometimes supplemented by a Service Level Agreement ("SLA") which sets out how the administrator will carry out its functions in a practical sense.

The Administration Agreement generally covers the following areas: services, fees and expenses, liability and indemnity, termination, and AML. The Administration Agreement is generally governed by and construed in accordance with the laws of the location of the administrator itself. However, the parties must agree which jurisdiction would more appropriately govern the agreement and any dispute arising in connection with it.

Services provided by the administrator usually include:

❑ registrar and transfer agency functions, such as processing subscription, redemption and transfer requests, as well as maintaining the share register;
❑ NAV calculation;
❑ preparation of financial statements and reports, including liaising with the fund's auditors;
❑ trade settlement support with fund managers or prime brokers; and
❑ ongoing support and review in relation to matters such as compliance and regulation.

The Administration Agreement should specify the level of fees payable to the administrator in respect of the administration services, and how the fees are calculated, accrued and paid. It is of note that the administrator is indemnified against any loss incurred as a result of the performance of its duties under the Administration Agreement, unless the loss or damage resulted from the administrator's fraud, negligence or wilful default.

The SLA sets out detailed operational flows and should, where possible, provide measurable objectives for all parties, such as setting out the precise trade reporting responsibilities and time deadlines. The prevailing objective of an SLA is to ensure that the fund administration process is documented and achievable with satisfactory administration service being delivered, however the SLA should also make possible the easy identification of problems.

Calculating NAV

Calculating the NAV of the fund on a correct and a timely basis is the most important function performed by the administrator, because the price at which investors buy and sell the shares or units of the fund is based on its NAV. NAV is also the key determinant in calculating the fees that the manager earns. Often the values of underlying investments of a hedge fund are highly subjective. Whilst both the fund and the administrator get current prices from the prime broker or executing brokers who handle their trades, or from other sources, a manager may try to override the price provided by the brokers, particularly for illiquid and hard to value securities such as bank debt. This can result in mispricing of the fund's portfolio and related regulatory action.

Historically in the US, unlike in the Europe, the administration function has been performed internally by the manager, and not by an independent administrator. It is therefore of note that the SEC has in recent years taken action against managers who deliberately overstated the value of the fund portfolio. In *Beacon Hill*, the SEC alleged that at various times Beacon Hill reported NAV and corresponding returns to fund investors that it knew or should have known were materially overstated.[6] Beacon Hill managed three feeder funds, as well as a master fund through which the feeder funds conducted trading. The funds principally invested in the mortgage-backed securities markets on a leveraged basis. SEC took further action in June 2004[7] when it sought to expand its case against Beacon Hill, and to charge four principals of Beacon Hill with fraud. The amended complaint alleged that the four principals of Beacon Hill together implemented a fraudulent scheme that resulted in investors losing more than US$300 million, by making material misrepresentations to investors and engaging in other fraudulent conduct. The misrepresentations concerned the methodology Beacon Hill used for calculating the NAV of the hedge funds it managed, the hedging and trading strategy for the purportedly market neutral funds, and the value and performance of the funds. It is, therefore, paramount to impress the importance of the administrator's independence throughout the valuation process. To alleviate similar concerns, there is now a move towards appointment of independent administrators in the US.

Before it can calculate the NAV the administrator must build up the trade history of the fund to acquire an accurate picture of the fund's assets. The administrator should also obtain from an independent source, whenever possible, the relevant and current prices to work out the value of the assets in the fund's portfolio. In order for the administrator to gain confidence that its record of the fund's holdings and prices is accurate, reconciliations with the statements provided by the prime broker, custodian or the manager must be performed. Finally, fees will be calculated and the NAV finalised. Thus, there are five basic steps in the calculation of NAV:

(a) trade capture;
(b) security pricing;
(c) reconciliations;
(d) expense calculation; and
(e) NAV calculation and reporting

which are considered in more detail below.

Trade capture

There are two basic types of transactions that an administrator will needs to process: transactions reflecting investor activity and those that reflect trading activity. As most hedge funds only allow subscriptions and redemptions on an infrequent basis (eg, monthly or quarterly) and tend to be aimed at high net worth or institutional investors, the investors' activity is less voluminous than that in other types of investment funds.

The trading activity of the fund must be timely and properly reflected in the valuation systems of the administrator as soon as possible. The most efficient way for the administrator to obtain an up-to-date trading history is to receive the trade reports directly from the prime broker with reports from the manager and if possible, fund counterparts and executing brokers. This is also seen as the best way of preserving the administrator's independence from the manager. In order to maintain the integrity of data, it is important that the administrator has the ability to capture trade and position files in an automated manner and is able to implement automated reconciliations of these data. When the files have been received and automatically uploaded on to the administrator's system, so as to minimise the risk of error, the administrator should the positions held by the fund. In other words, the number of securities held by the fund (long or short) in each position needs to be calculated and reconciled to the broker records. Once this has been completed, the administrator knows the assets of the fund, the holdings and the remaining cash. The next step is to apply prices to those assets in order to value them.

Security pricing

Generally security pricing is a high-risk area for administrators and managers, as well as the prime brokers. It requires high quality data feeds, automated price validation systems and highly experienced staff. There is always the risk of applying the wrong; or state prices to a fund with the potential for liability to the administrator and the fund.

It is generally straightforward for the administrator to capture the price of equity and fixed income securities if they are quoted or regularly traded, as their prices are publicly available. OTC and unquoted securities are harder to price and the administrator generally must obtain the counterparty valuation, as it is a good indication of the value of the position because often only the counterparty can release the fund from the position. Whilst in some jurisdictions the administrator is obliged to value the position based on the counterparty's valuation, in some cases, the administrator may be required to rely on prices determined by the manager, using the administrator's own pricing model for some specific complex derivatives instrument.

As previously stated, the administrator's independence from the manager and the prime broker is important, and the administrator must independently price the assets of the fund. The pricing process needs to be thorough so as not to expose the investors to the risk of incorrect pricing. What's more, only when the administrator is acting with apparent independence, can it safeguard the independence of the NAV process and protect the manager from accusations of bias. Despite this, there will be occasions when valuations of certain instruments can only be made by reference to or assistance from the manager and, as a last resort, the directors.

Reconciliations

It has been argued that the administrator's work only starts when the prices are captured. Once captured, the prices need to be validated or checked. All assets held by the fund should be reconciled between the administrator's records and those of the relevant third parties, including assets or collateral held with prime brokers, counterparties or custodians. The reconciliations should encompass nominal holdings, value and transactions entered into during the period. The administrator should be able to show that the prime broker is reflecting the same trades, holding the same positions and valuing those positions in line with the administrator's own records. Any material inconsistencies in reconciliation must be resolved before the NAV can be finalised.

Expense calculation

Although often overlooked, calculation of the expenses in the fund is also important. The fund should accrue its expenses on a timely basis so that it has sufficient accruals to meet expenses as they fall due. Administrators should accumulate all known variable fees, including management, administration, custody and performance fees, and fixed fees, such as audit fees, listing expenses, establishment costs, legal expenses and directors' fees. From the manager's perspective, the most important fee is the performance fee, but the performance fee is also important to investors because it directly influences the value of their investment.

It is a relatively common practice in the US for the managers to elect to defer receipt of their fees for a period of up to 10 years, in order to defer tax liabilities. In these cases, the fees are usually rein-vested into the fund. The administrator must ensure that this is accounted for properly.

NAV calculation and reporting

The final step is to calculate the NAV per share of each class in issue. This typically involves the following steps:

❑ calculate the allocation ratio for each class in issue;
❑ allocate the income, expenses, gains and losses for the fund based on the above allocation ratio;
❑ adjust for any share class specific items, such as hedge gain/loss, new issue profits, differing management and performance fees;
❑ calculate the NAV per share; and
❑ distribute the NAV.

NAV must then be properly allocated between classes of shares or feeder funds, and it must also accommodate class-specific items such as currency hedging or new issue trading.

When a dealing cycle is completed, a share dealing report should be produced, showing the total movement in capital and shares. This report should be used as an overall control on the deal-ing process and the total number of shares on the register should equal the total number of shares on the share dealing report.

The administrator should be in a position to provide other *ad hoc* reports such as an analysis of investors and their percentage hold-ings, investor activity levels over the life of the fund and NAV track record, in addition to advising the manager if any investors need to provide further compliance or taxation information.

In view of the range and complex nature of the services per-formed by the administrator, the relationship between the adminis-trator and the prime broker, which is not governed by a contract, written or oral, is critical.[8] In the first place, each needs to be fully aware of the other's requirements and processes. For example, the administrator depends on a high quality feed of trade information from the prime broker to understand what the fund holds at the given time and what therefore drives the valuation of the fund. Faulty data (or material data delivered late) leads to incorrect valu-ation and pricing, which in turn leads to incorrect creation and cancellation prices for shares and inaccurate assessment of the manager's performance entitlement. And a small slip can lead to a mistake of a substantial magnitude that can *in extremis* subvert the entire structure of the fund.

What if the data flow to the administrator is faulty or delayed, leading to an adulteration of the value calculations which the administrator carries out? If the Fund should lose money, or fail altogether, then the fund or its liquidators or potentially, if a duty of care could be shown to exist, aggrieved current (and former) investors might instigate legal action against the administrator. If the administrator wants to implicate the prime broker it will need to join it as a party to the proceedings. Again, no contract means suing in tort for negligence, which gives rise to uncertainty regarding applicable jurisdiction and legal forum.

Clearly, in the absence of a direct contractual relationship between the prime broker and the administrator, the prime broker should at the least have an active understanding of the administrators' particular role requirements in the relevant fund structure, and, ideally, the administrator should establish a clear *modus operandi* which may include some form of service standards for prompt and dependable performance of the prime broker's functions.

AML and KYC obligations

As discussed above, Cayman funds are subject to Cayman Islands AML provisions, however the fund will often delegate most of its account opening functions to the administrator. If the administrator is located in an equivalent jurisdiction, such as Ireland (where much fund administration business is based), compliance by the Administrator with its home state AML regulations would be deemed as compliance with the Cayman requirements. A fuller description of the typical AML requirements in force (at least those pertaining to the UK) is set out later in this chapter but, in essence, the administrator is required to verify the identity of any applicants subscribing for shares in the fund and sources of funds. Accordingly, each applicant must provide verification of identity to the satisfaction of the administrator. If the administrator (or any person for that matter) suspects that a payment to the fund whether by way of subscription or otherwise, is the proceeds of crime, the administrator is required to make a report to the relevant authorities.

Although the prime broker will not have relationships at the investor level, the prime broker itself is nevertheless subject to its own AML requirements and should be aware of such requirements as it services the day to day trading strategy of the fund.

THE EXECUTING BROKER

While some the prime brokers control the trading of the fund through provision of the key functions of executing, funding and clearing of trades, some funds opt not to have their execution and prime-brokerage services consolidated under one roof. An obvious reason for choosing a different executing broker is the cost of trade commission.

In instances where trades are executed by an executing broker, an agreement, which governs the relationship between the prime broker and the executing broker, must be in place. The agreement should set out the terms and conditions under which the executing brokers will be authorised to accept orders from the fund for settlement by the prime broker, as well as the logistics of trade reporting. Generally, the prime broker should accept for clearance and settlement trades executed only by the executing brokers designated by the fund. The best execution obligation in relation to the execution of trades for the fund would fall on the executing broker, and not the prime broker. While currently the fund as an intermediate customer can opt out of this entitlement, however, this will not be possible under MIFID.

In addition to fulfilling any regulatory requirements regarding notification of the fund as the client (usually via the manager), the executing broker should also notify the prime broker of all executed trades. This is important, as the prime broker would ordinarily be required to feed the trade reports directly to the administrator (as well as the fund's manager) to enable the administrator to reconcile trades and calculate the NAV.

It is therefore important that the relationship between the prime broker and any designated executing brokers be well defined and thorough to ensure that the information is provided to the prime broker in a timely fashion and in as much details as is possible in the circumstances. It appears to be a growing trend for the information to be fed though electronically from the executing brokers' database directly to the prime broker, so as to eliminate possibility of human error in collating and transmitting of the information.

THE CUSTODIAN OR SUB-CUSTODIAN

While ordinarily the prime broker would act as the custodian for the reasons discussed earlier, in some jurisdictions, particularly those in the European Union, there may be a regulatory require-ment to appoint a custodian in addition to a prime broker. The cus-todian may be required to review or oversee any rehypothecation employed by the prime broker, which would involve monitoring how much of the hedge fund's assets are exposed to the credit-worthiness of the prime broker.

The regulatory regime for funds using prime brokers typically requires that fully paid securities not used as collateral be main-tained in segregated accounts, whilst those acquired on margin or for which financing has been provided are not segregated and are available to the broker to use for its own purposes. The overall activity of the fund and the contractual agreement between the parties will dictate whether that is to be the case. In the UK and Ireland, securities are available to the prime broker, while in the US there are limitations on the amount of fund assets a prime broker can use/rehypothecate, by reference to the value of the fund's obligations to the prime broker.

In the instances where an appointment of a custodian is required by regulation, the custodian would ordinarily appoint the prime broker as a sub-custodian in the Custody Agreement between the custodian and the fund. The prime broker would take possession of the assets as it would do ordinarily in the absence of the third part custodian, in order to facilitate cash and stock lending, or sim-ply to provide custodial services should it need to facilitate the movement of collateral.

Quite apart from any such regulatory requirement, it is entirely open to the fund to appoint a third party custodian who can sup-port other arrangements of the fund that are not facilitated by the prime broker, such as holding physical securities for which the prime broker is not equipped to provide custody. In such instances, the custodian fulfils the functions of a traditional custodian of assets. The fund which engages in a foreign currency hedging strategy in a master–feeder structure at a feeder level, may also appoint a custodian to settle and execute the necessary foreign exchange transactions through its own books, if the prime broker maintains only the assets at the master level. The fund may maintain accounts with more than one prime broker, and may wish to appoint a custodian as a cash collection or clearing agent, initiating the transfer of funds between the prime brokers and paying out fees and expenses of the fund from a directly maintained cash reserve. In such circumstance, usually one prime broker is deemed the lead or clearing prime broker and monies will be moved into and out of the fund, or master fund, account held with the prime broker, who will settle with the other brokers on the basis of payment against delivery.

The prime broker may also sub-contract its custodial responsibility to its affiliate, or even a third-party entity, if so permitted under the contract. Under such circumstances, the prime broker would be required to act prudently in selection of a third-party custodian, but unless the Agreement expressly provides to the contrary, the prime broker would only take responsibility for those sub-custodians that are its affiliated entities, and not the third-party sub-custodians.

In any case, the prime broker's reported holdings should be reconciled to the fund's entire portfolio at each valuation point regardless of whether some securities are held by an independent custodian.

THE RISK MANAGER

A fund's primary goal in relation to risk control is to avoid structural risks, and the delivery of the strategic risk profile that investors require. Careful due diligence minimises these risks through analysis of the business model, whereas manager diversification mitigates the residual ones.

The asset allocation decision arguably has the single biggest impact on the risk profile of a fund. Careful due diligence and risk monitoring should provide a sufficient insight into the risk profile of fund investments. For example, funds with directional strategies are primarily exposed to market risks, whilst non-directional funds are more susceptible to liquidity risk. Managed accounts are an ideal platform for ongoing risk management for funds employing strategies that exhibit adequate liquidity and offer full transparency without putting their returns at risk. Real-time access to the portfolio enables appropriate actions to be taken on a daily basis. For strategies that exhibit listed liquidity or that require a certain level of confidentiality, fund investments represent the most efficient way of gaining exposure to a particular strategy.

Some funds appoint independent risk managers to assess the risks associated with the selected investment strategies. The need for a risk manager who is independent from the prime broker and the fund is amplified by the fact that in addition to the market and credit risks, the risk manager must take into account the operational risk in the light of the fund's portfolio being held by the prime broker.

The risks within the portfolio have to be monitored and managed extensively at the fund level through the risk manager, in order to obtain early warnings of style drifts and performance deterioration. Risk monitoring is the process of measuring the degree of risk inherent in a given portfolio, and hence it is a passive backward-looking approach much like an accounting view. Risk management is more than risk monitoring, as it employs one set of risk measures to allocate risk optimally among various assets and uses another type of risk measure to monitor exposures and make adjustments in a liquid fund. The way risk exposures are controlled depends on the type of investment. For directional strategies, VAR analysis, which can be performed at different levels of aggregation and along various dimensions, allows a consistent measurement of market and credit risk across instruments. Additional stress testing may assist in the assessment of the portfolio's sensitivity to adverse scenarios, particularly for investment strategies prone to liquidity risk.

THE EXCHANGES

Prime brokers need to be members of the LSE in the UK, and similar arrangements exist in other EU jurisdiction, as well as the US, in order to partake in trading activities on same. As members of the exchange, prime brokers are bound by the exchange rules, and are subject to monitoring and administrative sanctions which may be taken by the exchange for breach of the rules. In the UK, a prime broker will need to be a member of the LSE if it is providing the full executing and clearing/settlement services, but also if it is only involved in clearing activities.

THE REGULATOR

Over recent years, prime brokerage business has grown together with hedge fund management activity. Typically, a prime broker is an investment bank, regulated by the FSA. In addition institutional investors, including many pension funds, are increasingly investing in hedge funds, making the fund's managers as well as their related activities, including the functions carried out by prime brokers subject to increased attention from the regulator in the UK as well as across the EU and the US.

In the UK, as an authorised person under the FSMA 2000, a prime broker is subject to the FSA's Principles for Business, namely:

❏ *Integrity*: A firm must conduct its business with integrity.
❏ *Skill, care and diligence*: A firm must conduct its business with due skill, care and diligence.
❏ *Management and control*: A firm must take reasonable care to organise and control its affairs responsibly and effectively, with adequate risk management systems.
❏ *Financial prudence*: A firm must maintain adequate financial resources.
❏ *Market conduct*: A firm must observe proper standards of market conduct.
❏ *Customers' interests*: A firm must pay due regard to the interests of its customers and treat them fairly.
❏ *Communications with clients*: A firm must pay due regard to the information needs of its clients, and communicate information to them in a way which is clear, fair and not misleading.
❏ *Conflicts of interest*: A firm must manage conflicts of interest fairly, both between itself and its customers and between a customer and another client.
❏ *Customers: relationships of trust*: A firm must take reasonable care to ensure the suitability of its advice and discretionary decisions for any customer who is entitled to rely upon its judgement.
❏ *Clients' assets*: A firm must arrange adequate protection for clients' assets when it is responsible for them.

❑ *Relations with regulators*: A firm must deal with its regulators in an open and cooperative way, and must disclose to the FSA appropriately anything relating to the firm of which the FSA would reasonably expect notice.

These principles underlie the detailed conduct of business rules of the FSA and the manner in which the prime broker is required to provide its services across a range of hedge fund clients with varying (and potentially conflicting) strategies. Principle 11 effectively means that prime brokers based in the UK and subject to the FSA's regulation, are responsible to the FSA and may be called upon to provide information about a hedge fund even if the fund is domiciled off-shore and regardless of whether or not the manager is regulated. Any confidentiality agreement with the fund takes account of the prime broker's requirement to provide information to the regulator if so required.

In a discussion paper[9] on the risks associated with hedge funds, the FSA deliberated on whether it should consider differentiating prime brokers from other types of regulated entity by for example, creating a modifiable event under the FSA Handbook, or requiring them to obtain a specific permission from the FSA before undertaking such activity. Having considered the responses the FSA revealed[10] that it does not intend to take forward the option of a specific permission or notification for prime brokers. The FSA has indicated that it was persuaded that the more useful approach to those institutions that have prime broker characteristics is through the current close and continuous relationship these institutions have with their supervisors.

The FSA's prudential relationship with a typical prime broker means that the FSA has an interest in the counterparty relationships between hedge funds and the prime broker firms it supervises. The FSA conducts a regular "hedge funds as counterparties" survey among the major prime brokers, in order to enhance its understanding of prime brokerage and to gather data on the exposures of the firms to major hedge funds, either via prime brokerage or via the trading of other securities such as credit derivatives. These surveys complement ongoing work by supervisors and sector analysts to assess the quality of the firms' counterparty risk management to hedge funds and other counterparties. In addition, the FSA supervisors of prime brokers also consider counterparty risk management of hedge funds, as well as the management of conflicts of interest.

This increased attention paid by the FSA to the counterparty risk hedge funds pose to the prime brokers' prudential position may bring about a paradoxical result. In order to minimise their counterparty risk the prime brokers may be tempted (or arguably required) to adopt a policy of "when in doubt, close-out" in relation to its hedge fund clients, where the prime broker closes-out on an anticipated default prematurely. Such action would undoubtedly ruin the fund and cause losses to its investors, a result that the FSA would most likely prefer to avoid.

EMERGING REGULATORY TRENDS

Several hedge fund scandals that resulted in losses to investors have received public attention in recent years. The SEC has pursued 51 cases against US based managers that defrauded hedge fund investors or used the fund to defraud others, in amounts estimated at US$1.1bn over a five-year period.[11]

It is, therefore not surprising that regulators in many jurisdictions are devoting greater attention to hedge funds as a whole. Regulators are now focusing on all relationships with a structural matrix of a fund, including the administrator, prime broker and the manger, and not just the fund *per se*, and exploring how the responsibilities should be allocated and demarcated.

In October 2004, the SEC amended its rules and adopted a new rule under the Advisers Act to make registration mandatory for hedge fund managers with assets under management of over US$25m. This rule came into effect in February 2006, but was overturned in *Goldstein*. On 7 August 2006, the Chairman of the SEC announced[12] that the SEC would not appeal this decision, as discussed in a 10 August 2006 no-action latter, hedge fund managers who were required to register under the hedge fund adviser registration rules and who wish to de-register will be able to do so by filing appropriate forms, provided they do not hold themselves out to the public as investment advisers and under the Advisers Act s.203(b)(3) have no more than 14 clients (counting each fund and managed account as a client).

The SEC is, however considering new measures for overall regulation of hedge funds. Among the new proposals is a new anti-fraud rule which would have the effect of "looking through" a hedge fund to its investors. This would reverse the side-effect of the *Goldstein* decision that the anti-fraud provisions apply only to "clients" as the court interpreted that term, and not to investors in the hedge fund.[13] The SEC Chairman further emphasised that:

> *"... notwithstanding the Goldstein decision, it is important to point out that hedge funds today remain subject to SEC regulations and enforcement under the antifraud, civil liability, and other provisions of the federal securities laws. The SEC will continue to vigorously enforce the federal securities laws against hedge funds and hedge fund advisers who violate those laws. Hedge funds are not, should not be, and will not be unregulated".*[14]

Following this SEC announcement discussed above, the UK Alternative Investment Management Association ("AIMA") urged the SEC to permanently remove the requirement for non-US hedge fund managers also to register in the US, if they are already fully regulated in efficient jurisdictions, such as the UK and France.[15]

In the UK also, increased regulation of the hedge fund industry as a whole seems to be an emerging trend. Last year the FSA established the Hedge Fund Managers Supervision team, whose activities will be guided by the identified risks in line with the FSA's standard risk-based approach, and it has reviewed those prime brokers that have exposures to hedge funds through a survey[16] that explores management of counterparty credit relationships with hedge funds. As the FSA believes that it would be counter-productive if hedge fund managers re-located offshore where they would be subject to less oversight of their activities by the regulator, the FSA has increased contact with hedge fund managers in order to improve its understanding of the specific risks posed by the nature of hedge fund manager structures such as valuation processes. The FSA has commenced a thematic project to increase its understanding of industry approaches to pricing and valuation of less liquid and complex instruments, and intends to continue to monitor markets and systemic issues through its ongoing contact with the prime brokers, exchanges and other supervisors. The FSA is also considering the standards of appropriate disclosure in relation to side letters.

1 Note that hedge funds cannot be currently listed on the London Stock Exchange (LSE) but as listed on other exchanges including the Irish Stock Exchange and the Singapore Stock Exchange.

2 See paragraphs 4.1.6–4.1.10 of Annex 4 to the Draft Prudential Sourcebook for Bank, Building Societies and Investment Firms ("BIPRU").

3 This settlement has obtained in the UK with respect to institutional custody arrangements for a number of years. The investment Management Regulatory Organisation endorsed this logic in relation to its own rules for custody of assets under management by a UK-authorised manager, and the manner in which the UK-authorised manager must behave with respect to a third-party custodian is now determined in CASS 2.2.18R and subsequent provisions in the FSA's Client Assets Sourcebook.

4. See the discussion in Chapter 1.

5 With respect to the UK position, it is worth noting that COB 7.18 in the FSA's Conduct of Business Sourcebook comes fully into force as of June 2006, and serves to restrict the extent to which any broker can provide "bundled" services to his fund manager client where the overall fee covers the brokerage (which the manager wants) and a load of ancillary extras (which he may very well not). The extent to which research is provided must relate to the core brokerage service and not be contextually irrelevant to it. A fuller discussion of these arrangements is beyond the scope of this chapter.

6 See Litigation Release 17831/7 November 2002 at http://www.sec.gov/litigation/ litreleases/lr17831.htm

7 See also SEC Litigation Release 18745A/16 June 2004 at http://www.sec.gov/litigation/ litreleases/lr18745a.htm

8 The contract is with the fund. However, it is not unlikely that the manager will be the proactive entity in relation to pursuing an ineffective administrator. If the contract is for some reason subject to English law, then the Contracts (Third Party Rights) Act 1999 can be used to provide rights of action for specified third parties, such as the manager (circumventing the old doctrine of privity that underpinned English contract law for centuries).

9 DP05/4 – Hedge funds: A discussion of risk and regulatory engagement, June 2004, Q5.

10 See FS 06/2 Hedge funds: A discussion of risk and regulatory engagement – Feedback on DP05/4.

11 Advisers Act Release 2333, 69 FR 72054 (10 December 2004).

12 Statement of Chairman Cox Concerning the Decision of the U.S. Court of Appeals in Phillip Goldstein, *et al* v. SEC; 2006-135; 7 August 2006, http://www.sec.gov/news/press/ 2006/2006-135.htm

13 ibid.

14 ibid.

15 "AIMA Calls on SEC to Remove Dual Registration Requirement", *Hedgeweek*, 11 August 2006, at www.hedgeweek.com?articles/detail.jsp?content_id=30736

16 "Hedge Funds as Counterparties Survey" see FS 06/2 Hedge funds: A discussion of risk and regulatory engagement – Feedback on DP05/4.

5

The Legal Underpinnings of the Relationship: The "Level Playing Field"

Mark Berman

Editor, SEC Regulation Outside the US

INTRODUCTION

In this chapter, we discuss the key documents that define and give shape to the legal relationship between hedge funds and prime brokers. This involves the prime brokerage agreement, ISDAs, the Request for Proposal ("RFP") process and the Offering Materials. It touches on side letters (not a part of the hedge fund–prime broker relationship but relevant to hedge funds and their directors) and comments on ensuring that the agreements that each of the major service providers (prime broker, investment manager and administrator) are consistent and are subject to active oversight by the directors (or, in the LLP model, the general partner). The hedge fund–prime broker relationship is shaped, also, by applicable legal and regulatory requirements, including the hedge fund's jurisdiction of incorporation. Tax, accounting and audit considerations are dealt with in Chapter 8.

When does the hedge fund–prime broker relationship begin? It begins when the promoters take the decision to start the fund. It is at this point that the hedge fund's strategy is formulated, that investor profiles are drafted, that markets and instruments are identified and that the process to retain service providers, including the prime broker(s) begins. Many documents are generated at this stage, but among the most important of them is the RFP. A strong RFP, thorough responses by the prime broker prospects and meaningful due diligence by the promoter and the directors helps to ensure that all relevant issues are identified and discussed, that requirements are clearly stated (and discrepancies addressed) and that the relationship begins on the basis of trust and matched expectations – a level playing field. A weak RFP or no RFP at all may lead to conflicting expectations, misunderstandings and an unlevel playing field. It might hurt the fund's ability to trade or engage in certain activities or even lead it to add a second prime broker or to change prime broker.

The most important document that a hedge fund director signs or takes responsibility for, other than the Offering Materials and the constitutional documents, is the PBA. It is critical to get this document "right", just as it is crucial to select the "right" prime broker or prime brokers. For several years, prime brokers were selected by referral, through a prior relationship, on the basis that *this* bank or broker was in the best position to source securities to borrow in a certain jurisdiction, by reputation, by former employees going back to the firm from whence they came and because the prime broker commands a large market share and can deliver cost-effective lending and financing in multiple markets through an extensive network of sub-custodians. Prime broker agreements were usually signed on an "as is" basis and with little negotiation. Today, the factors noted above remain important considerations, but the selection of prime brokers is increasingly made through the RFP process and documents are negotiated before they are signed – in some cases, negotiations form part of the RFP process. Not to conduct an RFP process to select a prime broker on the basis of relevant requirements, the potential for growth, the ability to provide access to key markets and on the basis of a carefully negotiated agreement that reflects a "level playing field" is, some would argue, to hinder the ability of the hedge fund to operate effectively and to cede control of key aspects of the relationship to the prime broker.

Successful prime broker–hedge fund relationships are the product of meaningful negotiations and dialogue. Prime brokers provide valuable services for hedge funds. Without prime brokers, there would not be hedge funds as we know them today.

SELECTING THE PRIME BROKER
From inception to RFP

The directors are responsible for the hedge fund and are accountable to investors – they select the prime broker and oversee its relationship with the hedge fund and with the other service providers. The prime broker is the source of securities and funds, and the facilitator of trading. The investment manager manages the portfolio. The administrator keeps track of activities, values the portfolio and calculates the NAV and the NAV per Share. (In an LLP structure, the general partner would perform one or more of the manager/administrator/director roles.) The agreements between the hedge fund and each of these service providers must be clear on what each is required to do. The directors must be able to exercise oversight over each service provider, individually and as they relate to each other.

The process of selecting a prime broker should begin at the time when the decision to launch the hedge fund is taken. If it occurs later, the process is bound to become complicated by having to consider fundamental issues close to the launch, to renegotiate key points or to amend draft Offering Materials – all of which take time and cost money. It might also result in having to take a PBA on unacceptable or unnegotiated terms and with a promise to re-consider points later, an event that may never transpire. At this time, the nascent hedge fund, by its directors or promoter (or general partner), and with advice from the investment manager and counsel, should be taking a number of decisions, including the following key points:

❑ setting its strategy – aggressive growth, event driven, relative value, market neutral-hedging, multi strategy, special situations, and so on;

❑ identifying the investment objectives, policies and restrictions and setting parameters for capacity – and confirming that the administrator will monitor these;

❑ agreeing the types of instruments for trading and for hedging – by class, sector and geographic location;

❑ fixing policies and procedures for valuations and NAV calculations;

❑ identifying potential classes of investors – institutional investors only or institutions plus pension/benefit plan monies and, for non-US hedge funds, US investors or not;

❑ confirming countries where the hedge fund may be marketed;

❑ agreeing the structure – single entity or a master–feeder with one or more feeder funds;

❑ determining whether to list the hedge fund or an offshore feeder fund;

❑ identifying an administrator that could satisfy the hedge fund's requirements and that can work with the prime broker and other service providers;

❑ gauging the ability of the manager to achieve the investment objectives and policies and trade within the investment restrictions;

❑ deciding whether to use one or possibly two prime brokers.

These points help the directors build a profile of the type of prime broker that is required. For example, it may not be appropriate for a long/short European single entity fund that is managed in Paris and that wishes to use derivatives only for hedging to retain a prime broker that customarily services fixed income or global currency funds, or that is US-based and SEC regulated. A global long-short fund will require a prime broker that can deliver cost-effective global custodial services and where the responsibility for unaffiliated third party sub-custodians is spelt out.

It is for the directors of the hedge fund to select the prime broker (or the general partner), not the investment manager – although its views, as well as those of the administrator, need be taken into account in the decision-taking process. Directors may authorise a manager to conduct an RFP process on their behalf, but the decision to select or not to select rests with the directors. Ceding the decision-making authority not only sets a precedent by which the investment manager "controls" the fund but may lay the groundwork for a tax authority, such as HMR&C, to take the position that the hedge fund is "onshore" (doing business in the jurisdiction where the investment manager is located) and to tax the hedge fund in that location – a point discussed in Chapter 8.

To narrow the field of candidates to two or three finalists from which to select, we find the first two documents that form the hedge fund–prime broker relationship – the RFP and the confidentiality agreement. It is through these that the prime broker obtains the proposal operating model for the hedge fund and submits its bid, the bid is considered, due diligence takes place, the PBA is negotiated, materials are prepared and submitted to the directors for them to select a prime broker. Getting it right at this stage avoids delays, minimises costs and keeps everyone on schedule.

Confidentiality agreement

A confidentiality agreement is a document that by its terms permits two or more parties to share confidential information and to maintain the confidentiality of such information. It is prudent not to release the RFP before the party issuing the RFP and negotiating the PBA and the candidate prime broker sign the confidentiality agreement. This ensures that funds provide RFPs and related information to prospective prime brokers without fear of misuse or onward dissemination. It is, generally, the directors that sign the confidentiality agreement or, if the hedge fund has not yet been incorporated, the investment manager taking on this role or counsel to the hedge fund.

The person conducting the RFP process should ensure that every prime broker seeking to reply to an RFP should sign an identical confidentiality agreement. At a minimum, the confidentiality agreement should provide clear and easily enforceable terms. These include: a definition of confidential information; who states what is or is not confidential information; the names of the persons at the prime broker or an affiliate who may receive information and for what purpose; for how long information is to remain confidential; the governing law and venue; narrow carve outs for the public or inadvertent disclosure of information (eg, already in the public domain); when a prime broker may be required to provide information to third parties (by a regulator or by legal compulsion); and what remedy is available in case of a breach (usually an injunction). A good confidentiality agreement must provide for what happens should the process end and the fund not be launched or the prime broker not be selected – to return or destroy the information and to ensure that any others that receive information do likewise. If a prospective prime broker does not win the RFP process, the information provided to it should remain confidential for at least two calendar years with clear prohibitions on its use. If a prime broker wins the mandate, then, and to the extent that the provisions of the PBA and the confidentiality agreement are not consistent, the confidentiality agreement should remain in force during the life of the relationship – possibly beyond the end of the relationship.

RFPs

The RFP process is used to define the hedge fund's requirements and to provide a framework on which a prime broker may bid for and, if it wins, negotiate the mandate – services, markets, products and costs. There is no generally agreed template for an RFP, but usually, it involves disclosure of the following features of the prime broker:

❑ type of legal entity, information on the group of companies, incorporation, experience as a prime broker and general information, including regulatory history;

❑ summary of current hedge fund clients by location, type of structure and type of strategy – subject to confidentiality;

❑ transactions supported and not supported;

❑ lending and margining capabilities, and limitations;

❑ insurance coverage;

❑ clearing and custodial abilities – in-house, by affiliates or non-affiliates (if the latter, the prime broker should provide a sample copy of an agreement it would have in place with a non-affiliate and state whether and to what extent it takes responsibility for the actions of sub-custodians);

❑ corporate actions capacity;

❑ credit policies and requirements for ancillary documents such as ISDAs (and CSAs);

❑ capital introduction capabilities and experience – through mailings or cap intro events;

❑ risk management, trade and transaction reporting and controls policies and procedures;

❑ administrators with whom the prime broker works and has not yet worked;

❑ current arrangements with proposed executing brokers;

❑ whether affiliates will be used to trade, clear or hold derivatives and, if so, in what countries and subject to what regulations;

❑ business continuity requirements;

❑ client support teams and abilities;

❑ fees, costs and charges;

❑ regulatory history;

❑ the circumstances under which it would provide seed capital;

❑ whether it has been terminated as a prime broker by other hedge funds;

❑ positions on key legal issues; and
❑ countries of operation and support – broken down by use of affiliates and non-affiliates.

Further, the key issues that the prime broker needs to address in its response include the following.

❑ What local country restrictions apply to the instruments the hedge fund proposes to trade? Are there restrictions on short selling, borrowing to fund purchases and securities lending? Are certain securities hard to borrow?

❑ Will the prime broker also be the custodian? If not, will it use affiliated or non-affiliated custodians? It should be responsible for affiliated custodians. How does it select unaffiliated third-party custodians or sub-custodians and to what extent would it monitor and accept responsibility for them?

❑ How will custodians hold securities? What are the local country risks for, netting, default, insolvency and/or bankruptcy?

❑ What type of security interest would the prime broker wish to take over the hedge fund's assets? In what country? Would the security interest be registered? How would it be enforced? What assets would be subject to the charge?

❑ How will the prime broker calculate margin? How would margin calls be made and how much time would the fund be given to satisfy calls? How much of a "cushion" would the prime broker wish to have over and above the assets actually securing the charge?

❑ Are there limitations on the prime broker ability to hypothecate the fund's assets?

❑ Is client money protection afforded? What is the local regulatory treatment of cash? Are cash management programmes available? May the hedge fund/investment manager sweep cash out of its account with the prime broker for investment elsewhere without penalty?

❑ Does the prime broker wish to have broad events of default and broadly drawn definitions of key terms, including act of insolvency?

❑ How narrow would the execution powers be? At what point could the prime broker turn a failure to pay into an event of default and effectively close the fund?

❏ If there were to be an ISDA, would the prime broker require a CSA or a Master Netting Agreement? If so, what positions would the prime broker require in the way of cross default, aggregation and so on? Would the prime broker seek wide additional events of termination in the ISDA, including NAV decline triggers or other events, credit driven or not, that would favour the prime broker?

❏ To what extent, if any, would the prime broker use affiliates by delegation or assignment? If this were to be the case, would the prime broker be responsible for their actions?

❏ How broadly would the indemnity, cross indemnity, disclaimer and liability clauses be drawn? What would be the triggers or carve outs in or for such clauses?

❏ Does the prime broker agree to criteria to measure its performance? Quarterly reviews?

❏ How would this prime broker wish to operate *vis-à-vis* a second prime broker? Does it require exclusivity?

❏ What provisions would govern termination by one or the other party?

The RFP process should be driven by a number of factors, including the following.

❏ The selection process should be driven on the basis of what the prime broker can and cannot provide – and what it will cost.

❏ The directors of the fund have the final say. The manager and administrator will be called on for their input on the options available to the fund, but for sound corporate governance purposes and to avoid adverse tax consequences, the decision rests with those responsible for the fund and accountable to the investors.

❏ The information in the RFP must be concise and cover all key points. Not to do this wastes time and invites delays to obtain clarification. It would result in the prime broker's bid for the mandate being inaccurate and possibly lead to a wrong choice or a decision to be taken on a factor that, when clarified, might lead to the need to amend documents (including the PBA and even the Offering Materials), to obtain shareholder consent to effect changes or even to add a second prime broker or change a current prime broker.

❑ A meaningful RFP process involves due diligence and competitive negotiations. It is prudent not to select a single finalist from among several candidates and then negotiate the PBA. The RFP process should involve interviews with hedge fund personnel at which time queries may be answered or points clarified. The process should then move to due diligence taking place at the prime broker's offices and with members other than the prime broker selling group. This would include credit, legal and compliance, documentation, trading, "cap intro" staff and senior management. The process would conclude in a final stage in which at least two finalist candidates negotiate the PBA and, if required, an ISDA or a CSA. The result of this is an integral part of the decision-making process.

The results of these steps should be documented and provided to the directors for their consideration at a duly quorate meeting of the board of directors. These materials should be accompanied by other key documents such as the Offering Materials, the Articles, the administration agreement and, if required, ISDAs and CSAs. At this meeting, the directors would query the proposal and address issues to ensure that their decision to appoint a prime broker is documented, well reasoned and appropriate to the needs of the fund.

The decision to select a prime broker should be set forth in a resolution of the directors at a duly quorate meeting. (The decision should not, unless exigencies are involved, be taken by one director under a power of attorney given to him or her by the other directors. If this is required, the directors must receive all documents to review when they receive the power to consider and sign, and any comments they raise must be documented and taken into account.) That resolution should:

❑ refer to all documents provided to the directors for their consideration;
❑ ensure that disclosures in all documents are complete and consistent;
❑ include a summary of the RFP process;
❑ provide a summary of the key points to be contained in the PBA and a comparison of how the agreement furnished by the proposed prime broker addressed these points;

❑ state the key issues considered in the selection process;

❑ identify the risks (if any) involved with the selection of this particular prime broker;

❑ approve the fee schedule for at least a 12-month period and the basis on which fees would be re-negotiated – up or down;

❑ give clear approvals – this entails approving specific documents (or if needed authorising a director or an approved agent to complete negotiations on a specific document), naming authorised signatories, providing time lines within which to complete steps prior to launch, approving the opening of accounts with the prime broker and addressing further issues;

❑ approve disclosures about the prime broker and the PBA in the Offering Materials; and

❑ authorise one director or a duly appointed agent to give such instructions, sign such documents and take such steps as are required to address issues arising between the date of this meeting and the next directors meeting.

THE PRIME BROKERAGE AGREEMENT

The PBA is the document that sets forth the legal relationship between the hedge fund and the prime broker. There are two basics types of PBAs (and further variations on each): the US model, which is driven by US legal requirements and is used by US entities (SEC registered broker-dealers and US banks) (*see* Chapter 2); and the international model that is used by non-US prime brokers.

Key issues

The PBA is signed by the hedge fund (by its directors or a duly authorised agent under a resolution or a power of attorney) and the prime broker. Often, in addition to a PBA, the hedge fund and the prime broker will put in place other documents, such as an ISDA (and schedule), a CSA, a general terms of business, a futures and options agreement (for listed instruments), account opening documents, local market trading documents (authorisations, proxies, applications, powers and appointments), securities lending agreements, certified true lists of authorised traders and persons to give instructions to move funds, executing broker agreements and any other documentation. Both parties will be required to provide each other with copies of resolutions, certificates of incorporation and other documentation. It may be the case that additional materials are required, such as US Internal Revenue Service tax forms (Forms W-8IMY, 8832 and SS-4), discussed in Chapter 8.

Who signs the PBA?

Normally, one entity provides prime brokerage services and it signs the PBA. However, many regional and global banks and broker-dealers offer prime brokerage by outsourcing certain operations or services to affiliates. In that case, the prime broker would sign for itself and for its affiliates as agent. If multiple entities sign, supporting documentation should be obtained. If one entity signs for itself and as agent for others, there should be an affirmative requirement on it to bring to the attention of the hedge fund any matters relevant to the performance of the agent or any change in status, and the sole signing entity should assume responsibility on an unqualified basis for the acts or omissions of any delegated agent.

Key terms

Every PBA raises significant legal issues (these are also applicable to the Offering Materials and, indeed, the hedge fund's strategy), and the most important of these are set out below, in the context of the international PBA model. The discussion overleaf is not exhaustive and is not intended be or to provide definitive advice, but serves as a starting point to negotiate and measure a PBA.

Definitions

Every definition must be clear and non-circular.

Act of insolvency: Prime brokers wish this to be as wide as possible and hedge funds want to narrow this, possibly to the definition applicable to it in its jurisdiction of incorporation. Hedge funds should accept a definition that is objective, linked to relevant jurisdictions and does not permit an act that on its own could not result, in an event that would close the hedge fund and permit a prime broker (or others) to liquidate the portfolio.

Assets: Generally, this refers to what securities and cash the prime broker holds for the hedge fund. (We use the term "Assets" to refer to cash and securities throughout the remainder of this chapter.) It is important to ensure that the security interest that the prime broker takes is over the assets that are actually required to satisfy the charge, not over the entire portfolio.

Event of default: A pivotal term. Prime brokers wish this to be as wide as possible and hedge funds want to narrow this. The occurrence of an event of default normally gives the prime broker the ability to cease operations, execute over assets subject to the security interest, liquidate the portfolio and return the balance, if any, to the hedge fund. Effectively, the occurrence of an event of default would close a hedge fund. The events that should comprise an event of default are acts of insolvency, fails to pay significant amounts (not just trades that fail to settle or are DK'd) material changes in the hedge fund's structure or finances that, in the prime broker's opinion, affect its ability to do business with the hedge fund defaults or events of default in other documents should be excluded. Events of default should be narrowly defined and be limited to events that do reasonably require a portfolio to be liquidated or the relationship to end.

ISDAs also contain a definition of "event of default", and caution must be taken to ensure that the definition in that agreement is, to the extent possible, identical to that in the PBA – and to avoid cross defaults.

Margin: A clear definition of what margin is, how to calculate it and who does the calculation is important. Margin is the amount of money or securities that the prime broker requires and that becomes subject to the charge. Accordingly, there must be a margin policy and, disclosure about what is and what is not subject to the charge and when margin is required (and all related calculations). Margin should be required when the value of the assets held by the prime broker, not all of assets of the hedge fund, drops to a point reasonably that is above or equal to the amount of the security interest in the portfolio. If the value of the assets held by a prime broker is, say, £240,000,000 and the prime broker has extended credit (cash and securities lent) in an amount equal to, say, £110,000,000, the security interest should cover only the amount of credit actually extended, plus costs, and the point at which margin is called should be just above the £110,000,000, high enough to cover sudden or large swings in the value of assets to protect the prime broker but low enough to ensure that the hedge fund keeps unencumbered assets free of the security interest and, also, free from margin calls.

NAV, NAV per Share and other defined terms: PBAs often contain definitions of these, and other terms (and provisions) that are defined and used in the Offering Materials or the Articles. In such cases, definitions should be identical to those in these other documents.

How are assets to be held

The manner in which assets are held is a function not only of what type of entity the prime broker is and how it is structured, but of the markets where assets are held, the type of assets, where the prime broker is incorporated and whether unaffiliated third parties hold cash and securities. It is preferable for the prime broker to hold cash subject to client money protection. Securities usually cannot be held in a segregated account in the name of the hedge fund; as such, they should be held in the name of the prime broker or its nominee or sub-custodian. Beneficial ownership should always remain with the hedge fund (save for jurisdictions where this is not legally possible and outright transfer of title is required), and the books and records of the prime broker should clearly reflect the hedge fund's ownership.

Use of excess cash

The hedge fund should be able to have its excess cash held at the prime broker free of the security interest and in an interest bearing account, or be able to sweep it without being subject to increased margin rates.

Fiduciary duties

Prime brokers may not wish to owe fiduciary duties to a hedge fund client. The hedge fund should attempt to have the prime broker owe these and, if this is not possible, agree at a minimum to have the prime broker owe a general duty of care and also enhanced duties for custodial functions. Duties of confidentiality should not be waived or compromised.

Hypothecation

There should be a clear statement of what assets the prime broker may hypothecate, and a stated maximum per cent of the assets that may be used. The assets that the prime broker may borrow, lend, sell or otherwise transfer for its use or for the use of its customers are those assets in the portfolio that are subject to the security interest. The figure of 100% of the assets encumbered by the security interest is usually the maximum benchmark. Prime brokers require a provision that permits them to receive any fee, profit or benefit that it achieves from rehypothecation. Hedge funds should realise that a prime broker that hypothecates assets is obligated to return "equivalent securities" (assets of an identical type, value and description).

Indemnities

Few clauses the collective attention of directors, lawyers and hedge fund managers than indemnity clauses. In essence, an indemnity clause provides a form of protection to a person that, in the proper course of its operations it becomes subject to a demand, claim or suit by third party and suffers a loss, it may seek reimbursement from a designated person for that loss. Prime brokers wish to have indemnity clauses drafted as widely as possible. Hedge funds, naturally, wish to limit them. A good balance to achieve in an indemnity clause would be to achieve the following:

❏ limit the clause only to the prime broker and its officers, directors and employees that actually perform services under the PBA ("indemnified persons");
❏ condition the giving of an indemnity on the absence of negligence, fraud, wilful misconduct or breach of the PBA by an indemnified person;
❏ clarify that the indemnity is limited to actual claims or losses that arise directly from the obligations of an indemnified person under the PBA, and for reasonable legal fees;
❏ avoid payment on demand provisions – these require payment to be made before a claim may be established and may involve large amounts of money that, should the claim not be established, may be irrecoverable.

Limitations of liability

Both hedge funds and prime brokers wish to limit their liability. Prime brokers and/or their employees, directors or officers performing prime brokerage activities should be liable in the event of negligence, fraud, wilful misconduct or breach of the PBA. Liability should extend to the material acts or omissions of affiliates of the prime broker to whom the prime broker delegates activities. Liability should also extend to unaffiliated third parties to whom the prime broker assigns its duties. Prime brokers accept liability for affiliates and try to narrow or eliminate liability as regards unaffiliated third parties. As the hedge fund would not be in privity of contract with the prime broker's delegatees, hedge fund directors should not permit a prime broker to escape responsibility for the acts or omissions of third parties to whom they delegate responsibilities under the PBA.

Generally, both parties agree not to be liable for consequential or indirect losses.

Unaffiliated third-party sub-custodians

Prime brokers assume liability for affiliated sub-custodians but do not wish to assume liability for the acts or omissions of unaffiliated third party sub-custodians (or for their insolvency or bankruptcy). Hedge fund directors require otherwise. A compromise position is for the prime broker to be responsible for hiring and monitoring unaffiliated sub-custodians, to agree to assist the hedge fund in recovery against third party unaffiliated sub-custodians and to assign claims that they have against such persons. Such a critical point should not be left to be discussed and agreed after the hedge fund starts trading or be subject to carve outs on a market by market basis.

Security interest

Prime brokers require a charge over the assets in the portfolio. Most take a fixed charge, while others also seek a floating charge. A fixed charge is a charge (security interest) over a particular asset. A floating charge is a charge that remains in place on a continuous basis over non-fixed assets, such as securities and cash, and that permits the grantor to deal freely with the assets. A combination of a fixed and floating charge provides the maximum amount of protection to the prime broker and may presents the greatest issues to the hedge fund in the case of an event of default. Security interests and the means to perfect, realise and enforce them vary from jurisdiction to jurisdiction.

Rights on default/execution provisions

Prime brokers wish to have a range of options available on the occurance of an event of default. These include a cessation of funding and lending activities, crystallisation of the security interest, portfolio sales/liquidation and the appointment of a receiver. No hedge fund director should grant such wide powers for all events. A compromise is attainable, in which both agree a threshold amount over which an event of default is declared and the rights on default come into play, and under which the sole remedy available to the prime broker is to use available cash or to agree to sell individual positions. Individual failed trades would not be events of default or give rise to rights on default. Many versions of the threshold amount formulation exist. Most involve a figure that is the "greater of" a fixed amount or a per cent of the hedge fund NAV, and usually start as the figure of £500,000 (or £1,000,000 for larger funds). Directors should ensure that there are provisions to reset the figure based on changes to the hedge fund AUM.

NAV decline triggers

NAV decline triggers provide that if the hedge fund's NAV (AUM) declines by a stated per cent in a rolling 12 month period, the counterparty may exercise certain rights or use such a decline to declare a termination event. NAV triggers also include NAV per Share decline triggers. NAV decline triggers rarely appear in PBAs and should be a point to negotiate away – both in the PBA and in an ISDA.

Termination

Prime brokers favour unilateral termination provisions that give them the right to close the prime brokerage account for cause, but also, on occasion, for no specific reason. Generally, a prime broker would use such a clause if it wished to curtail its activities in certain sectors, or for other reasons. Effective PBAs should have bilateral termination provisions, as hedge fund directors, may wish to terminate these agreements for poor service or in the event of a change in strategy and a move to a different prime broker. Procedures should be in place to permit either party to terminate not just for cause, but when legitimate business reasons either. Clear provisions should be in place for trading, portfolio handover, closeouts, information feeds and other matters from the time notice to terminate is served until after termination. Termination should not be an event of default and should be carved out of the definition of this term. A prime brokers liability under a PBA should not end when termination occurs.

Representations and warranties

Just as it is important for a prime broker to receive a warranty and representation that the hedge fund is validly formed and that the PBA will be a valid, legal and binding obligation enforceable by its terms, so, too, does the hedge fund needs such reps and warranties from the prime broker. Representations and warranties, whenever possible, should be bilateral and include key points such as incorporation, valid existence, execution, enforceability, agreement to make notification if certain events transpire, and so on. Certain reps and warranties are appropriate for one of the parties, such as the rep that the prime broker is duly authorised and regulated. Representations and warranties usually do not prevent significant issues but must be thought out and carefully drafted.

Cross margin, cross netting and cross default

Prime brokers, when putting in place multiple agreements (a PBA, an ISDA, an OSLA and/or a Global Master Securities Lending Agreement ("GMSLA")), wish to achieve cross margin, cross netting and cross default. These provisions provide the greatest credit protection to the prime broker. A hedge fund, particularly a new fund, may receive benefits from cross margining, but to agree to all three imposes severe risks. Today, industry practice is to negotiate for cross margin, cross netting, and cross default. Default provisions should not work "upwards" so that if an ISDA or a GMSLA is terminated that would result in the closure of positions under these agreements but not "rise up" to terminate the PBA itself. There are, however, valid reasons for "downward" terminations of ISDAs and other documents with the prime broker, but not other hedge fund counterparties.

Information barriers

Prime brokers are sophisticated entities that operate on a regional or global basis. They offer many services, in addition to prime brokerage. As regulated institutions, they are required to ensure that information that one department receives is ring-fenced so that it does not, save for narrow exceptions, flow to other departments. Passing information about a hedge fund's trading and positions is confidential information, should be done in limited instances – for risk credit compliance, internal audit, etc. PBAs and Offering Materials should make clear that the prime broker operates information barriers sufficient to ensure compliance with relevant legal and regulatory requirements and to ensure that information proprietary to the hedge fund is confidential and properly controlled.

Service level agreements

Hedge funds require service providers to enter into service level agreements (SLA) to provide a means to measure performance. SLAs, as they are known, should contain provisions for regular reviews. The trend is in favour of having SLAs with hedge funds, particularly when there are multiple prime brokers. SLAs should be signed by the parties to ensure enforceability.

RELATED DOCUMENTS
Offering Materials and verification notes

The Offering Materials are the document that is used to market shares or interests of a hedge fund. This document must contain a clear statement of the material terms of the PBA, together with summary information about the prime broker. If the prime broker or an affiliate contributes seed capital, this fact might have to be disclosed (if it is material).

The disclosure in Offering Materials required about a prime broker should touch on the following points:

- ❑ the identity of the prime broker and any affiliate providing duties by delegation;
- ❑ the actual services to be performed eg, custody, clearing, financing and reporting;
- ❑ a statement making clear what services will not be performed eg, investment advisory or discretionary management;
- ❑ the nature of the security interest over the assets in the portfolio;
- ❑ what monitoring, if any, is to be performed;
- ❑ events of default and how they would be exercised;
- ❑ termination provisions;

❑ calculation of fees; and
❑ any other relevant disclosures.

Prime brokers are often asked to sign verification notes in the lead up to the initial offering of shares or Interests. Verification notes, drawn up by outside counsel, provide a means to verify statements in the Offering Materials and ensure that disclosures in all documents are consistent. Prime brokers usually participate in aspects of the verification process and in most instances sign the notes.

Executing broker agreements

Hedge fund investment managers enter into executing broker agreements with their trading counterparts and with their prime brokers. Trades effected by the executing broker are given up to the prime broker to clear. Executing broker agreements not only provide the means by which trading and give ups take place, but they may impose an obligation on the manager to settle trades for its own account of the prime broker DK's a trade. Managers and their hedge funds should negotiate out of such provisions.

ISDAs

ISDAs are agreements that permit counterparties to trade derivative instruments with market-standard terms and conditions. It is rare for a hedge fund not to have even a single ISDA in place, as it will be inevitable that at some point the manager will wish to trade derivatives at least to hedge positions. Parties rarely negotiate the ISDA itself, but negotiate the ISDA schedule and the attendant CSAs. These are the subject of intense, time-consuming negotiations, often lasting weeks. Since timing is a critical element, ISDA Schedule negotiations need to commence as soon as practicable to ensure that any outstanding issues are address and resolved prior to the time that the PBA is tabled before the directors for their approval. There is a 2002 ISDA Master Agreement in use in the market, but many parties prefer to use the 1999 ISDA Master Agreement. Key terms are contained in the 2003 Definitions. It takes considerable time to understand the operation of ISDAs and to learn to negotiate them, and negotiation is best left to qualified in house counsel or documentation teams.

Caution must be exercised in trading derivatives and using ISDAs. ISDA confirmations may contain clauses that modify or replace provisions or figures in an ISDA Schedule. Operational personnel in managers and/or administrators must ensure that every ISDA confirmation is carefully checked to ensure that all terms are understood.

Among the important provisions of an ISDA schedule are the following.

Cross default: Cross default clauses provide that if a default occurs in relation to one document, other documents may be defaulted. As noted above, hedge funds should avoid cross default provisions, to help ensure that the termination of an ISDA under which there are few positions or many positions with relatively little value in comparison to the hedge fund's AUM or portfolio with the prime broker does not terminate all documents and effectively close the fund.

Additional termination event: These are events that, if they transpire, permit a counterparty to cease trading, liquidate positions, net payment obligations to a single payment owed by or to it and require that such payment be made or make such payment. Prime brokers and other hedge fund counterparties often seek additional termination events such as NAV decline triggers (discussed above), changes in financial condition, late delivery of key documents, failure to timely deliver monthly NAVs and NAV per Share figures, the loss of key manager employees, incorrect statements in documents, firing the manager and replacing it with a new manager that is not an affiliate or in the same group of companies and other provisions. Historically, hedge funds agreed to such provisions, but in the last few years there has been a trend not to include such terms – particularly as they represent credit protections for counterparties and prime brokers, and those entities are reluctant to provide similar provisions to hedge funds.

Threshold amount: This comes into play in the event of a default. When an event of default occurs, positions are closed and payments netted to achieve a single figure that is owed to the non-defaulting counterparty. If the defaulting counterparty owes the non-defaulting counterparty an amount that is greater than the threshold amount, this would kick off a cross default provision, resulting in the termination of other documents. If ISDAs are to contain threshold amounts and cross default provisions, care must be taken to negotiate a figure that the hedge fund realistically believes would, if defaults occurred, not jeopardise it.

Side letters

Side letters are enforceable agreements entered into by investors and hedge funds in order for the investor to obtain a benefit, right or concession that is not available to all investors and/or that would result in the investor receiving a favourable position. Provisions of side letters cover many issues, including: the provision of audited financial statements by certain dates; an exemption from early redemption fees; notification of the occurrence of certain events; preferable treatment in the event of certain conditions arising – nearly anything that might in some way give an investor a degree of leverage over other investors, first notice of events, preferential treatment or an economic advantage.

In order for a hedge fund to be able to issue a side letter, there must be appropriate authority in the Articles. If a hedge fund is listed for example, the ISE, the giving of a side letter may result in a breach of the requirement to treat shareholders equally. Hedge fund directors must understand that side letters raise significant legal and corporate governance issues. Directors must consider whether granting a side letter is consistent with their legal obligations and with the fiduciary duties that they owe. The terms of a side letter might result in an amendment to Offering Materials, or even the Articles, and might require not just the filing of mended documents, but also the public disclosure of the side letter – which would invariably be a breach of the confidentiality terms of the side letter itself.

Regulators are turning their attention to side letters.

The SEC is concerned that side letters raise conflicts of interest and result in preferential treatment to certain investors. In testimony in May 2006 before the Subcommittee on Securities and Investment of the US Senate Banking Committee on Banking, Housing, and Urban Affairs, Susan Wyderko, director of the SEC's Office of Investor Education and Assistance, stated that the SEC is looking at side letters during inspections. She testified that certain side letters "are more troubling because they may involve material conflicts of interest that can harm the interests of other investors. Chief among these types of side letter agreements are those that give certain investors liquidity preferences or provide them with more access to portfolio information. Our examination staff will review side letter agreements and evaluate whether appropriate disclosure of the side letters and relevant conflicts has been made to other investors."[1]

The UK FSA, in its FSA feedback paper, stated that side letters might contribute to a market failure.

"[S]ide letters result in some, often large, investors receiving more information and preferential (early) redemption terms compared with other investors in the same share class (who may be unaware of that side letters exist and who will be denied these terms). We believe that failure by UK based hedge fund managers, to disclose the existence of these side letters is, **amongst other potential breaches** in breach of Principle 1 of our Principles for Businesses ("a firm must conduct its business with integrity"). As with valuation abuses, we will take action on this basis. *As a minimum we would expect acceptable market practice to be for managers to ensure that all investors are informed when a side letter is granted and any conflicts that may arise are adequately managed.* Managers that fail to inform investors will need to carefully consider their position. We have concluded that it is important to review these practices later in 2006. That work will inform our policy thinking and enable us to take action against individual firms and their senior management if appropriate [emphasis supplied]."[2]

Side letters involve hedge funds and investors and touch tangentially on the hedge fund–prime broker relationship. A complete discussion of side letters is beyond the scope of this chapter, but it is worth pointing out some of the issues that they raise.

CONCLUSION

As noted at the outset of this chapter, successful prime broker-hedge fund relationships are the product of meaningful negotiations and dialogue. The efforts do not, however, cease or slow when the fund is launched. For the relationship to grow and bear fruit, both hedge fund and prime broker must find ways to ensure that their respective needs are clearly articulated. In all cases, requirements must be reduced to writing to ensure clarity and enforceability. Not do so would invite and a difficult relationship that might end in the termination of the relationship and, possibly, litigation. The RFP process, PBAs and related documentation not only record the terms of the agreement, but provide a structure on which to enhance the relationship.

1   Testimony Concerning Hedge Funds Before the Subcommittee on Securities and Investment of the US Senate Committee on Banking, Housing, and Urban Affairs, Susan Ferris Wyderko, Director, Office of Investor Education and Assistance, US Securities and Exchange Commission (16 May 2006).
2   FSA Feedback paper, at 6.

6

The Trading and Economic Factors Driving the Relationship

Paul Dentskevich

HSH Nordbank AG

INTRODUCTION

When asked to identify the key factors that drive their relationship with their prime broker(s), hedge fund managers may respond with many possible answers. On the whole, managers go about their business primarily concerned with trading issues (and continued growth in AUM) and do not wish to become involved with "issues at the edge", such as why something cannot be done, why something went wrong, why did that particular trade fail or why can't I borrow that stock. Key employees of the manager – the fund manager(s), the trader, the administration liaison and distribution and marketing staff – desire an environment where their efforts can focus on the priorities of executing their strategies in the most efficient manner, increasing Assets Under Management (AUM) and addressing investor queries smoothly and efficiently. The prime broker, in providing the needed funding, stock and cap intros, plus key risk management tools, is at the centre of nearly everything that the manager does.

THE "RELATIONSHIP" SIDE OF THE TRADING AND ECONOMIC FACTORS

During the life of a hedge fund, many factors will influence its relationship with its prime broker(s). These factors will wax and wan in importance and change or drop away, to be replaced by other issues.

Ultimately, economics is at the heart of the relationship. In the lead up to launch and in the early days of a hedge fund's life, securing assets under management sufficient to launch and to trade to start to deliver a respectable performance is the most pressing issue. The ability of the prime broker to introduce potential investors to the hedge fund and to secure initial investments helps set the tone for much that follows. Success may be measured not just from the volume/magnitude of investments but also from the correlation of claims made during the "courting" phase to launch and through the first year or two. Often, a relationship can be made, or soured, in the early days when claims of access to large number of potential investors eager to hear this hedge fund's story and invest does or does not materialise or leads to little or no investment. A related concern is a promise of seed capital from the prime broker itself that, in the course of the request for proposal (RFP) process and negotiations leading to the decision by the directors to retain that firm, comes in timely – or is a fraction of what was promised, is heavily conditioned, is delayed or does not come about.

Other factors that emerge at the beginning of the relationship are agreements to renegotiate fees during the first six months/one year, a promise of fee breaks in return for a commitment by the hedge fund not to change prime brokers or to retain a second prime broker for a defined period. When the fund begins to grow and during or at the end of the first year, the parties would hold an "assessment meeting" and the "economics" of the relationship would become a discussion point.

It is at this point that the parties will start to focus on one of the "core" elements of the hedge fund–prime broker relationship – "profits *vs* service" – and possibly act on it for the first time. The future direction and fate of the relationship might be defined at this time. A prime broker that balances fees and profits with service will retain this and other hedge fund clients. Rigidity in fees, a large number of failed cap intros, DK's trades, the quality of the advice and the efficiency with which *ad hoc* requests are satisfied may make or break the relationship.

DIFFERENCES BETWEEN PRIME BROKERAGE SERVICES
At present there is not a "one size fits all" approach to the services offered by prime brokers to the hedge fund industry at large. There

are extensive differences between the prime brokerage services for equity-related, fixed income or credit related hedge funds, and between prime brokers that service FX, commodity and futures-based funds.

Equity-related hedge funds are looking for easy financing of their trading activities, the ability to buy and sell stocks in an affordable manner. In its simplest form, financing is a floating rate line of credit (usually related to Libor); however, there are subtle variations on the theme. Some prime brokers offer gross pricing, which means that a hedge fund pays one rate for financing and receives a different, lower rate, for credit balances it maintains. Other prime brokers offer net pricing, which means that credit balances are offset against debit balances before determining financing charges. Proponents of gross pricing argue that it is more transparent, and that those that offer net pricing will simply recoup any benefits received by charging higher stock loan fees. In reality, the important point is that the hedge fund directors must clearly understand the charging structure before signing. It is advisable to compare the charges of various prime brokers based on different scenarios, eg, net long, net short to determine the most favourable charging structure.

Other features such as auto-borrow make life easy, although some versions of this are not quite automatic. This leads to delays in getting stock and impacts trading. Quite often it is in times of market dislocation or excessive volatility that issues concerning stock borrowing arise. The supply of "easy to borrow" stocks may slow or dry, leading to delays in settlement or DK'd trades. Another issue may be that fund managers do not check the list as thoroughly as they might, or not at all (thinking that there have not been changes to the list) and trade, to learn that stock cannot be timely delivered or to see that trades fail. Depending on the terms of the PBA, prime brokers may have an absolute right to DK trades without notice or for no reason, and a drying up of their supply of stock or a surge in borrowing a particular position might cause them strains that, in turn, impacts trading and results in an intra-day change to the "easy to borrow" list.

Fixed income prime brokerage formerly took the form of simply providing custodial services and financing obtained in the repo market. Generally, the prime broker would have an expectation that the majority of the hedge fund's repo trading would be through it, and the relationship would become strained when this was not the case. An increasing number of houses offer a fixed income equivalent to the services they offer to equity hedge funds. Prime brokers are also offering cash management, funding and FX services. The advent of intermediation has simplified many aspects of the functioning of the credit derivatives market: the costs can be quite significant and leave funds with a decision to either resource themselves or pay for the convenience.

ECONOMICS

As noted above, numerous economic factors have a direct influence on the relationship. What follows is a discussion of a few of the more prominent examples that may be provided by the prime broker and that shape the hedge fund's portfolio and returns – that may lead to gains and increased fees or even result in the creation of friction in the relationship. This list is by no means exhaustive, but helps to illustrate how certain economic factors influence the relationship, for the better and for the worse.

Trading equities *vs* CFDs

One of the hot topics in the UK is the question of whether to buy equities, CFDs or total return swaps. The cost of buying equities *vs* CFDs or swaps is more than just an issue of financing. In the UK, cash purchases of cash equities by investors (not intermediaries) attracts stamp duty, currently 50 bp. The more a hedge fund buys UK equities, the more stamp duty it pays and the more performance is affected. Using derivatives, total return swaps or CFDs to replicate the economic exposure of equities helps a hedge fund reduce its purchasing costs by eliminating the need to pay stamp duty. (The prime broker or executing broker would not be liable for stamp duty to the extent that it acquired the underlying position as an intermediary.) It is an attractive proposition to a hedge fund. It does, however, require the implementation of special arrangements and documentation by which the hedge fund's executing broker sells the derivative to the hedge fund while the prime broker or the executing broker (not the hedge fund) achieves the underlying equity to hedge its exposure. It also needs to be done in a manner that would not result in HMR&C taking the position that the procedure employed resulted in avoidance or evasion and assessing tax, interest or penalties. Considerable care needs to be taken in drawing up the documentation and implementing the procedures. The hedge fund should avoid any steps that might result in the prime broker or the executing broker putting any underlying equity back to the hedge fund.

It is worth adding a cautionary note about Ireland where the Office of Revenue Commissioners considered looking to prevent such types of arrangement. No action was taken, out of a desire to avoid having Irish equities become less competitive than UK stocks.

UK managers of hedge funds have made extensive use of CFDs. Estimates of the use of hedge funds trading CFDs have ranged as high as 50% of the market for this instrument in London. Trading CFDs may be economically sound, but may also lead to issues for managers that run long and long-short funds that each trade CFDs (the long only fund must be properly empowered to be able to trade these instruments at all). Trading CFDs for both long and long-short funds might result in issues under UK FSA rules (conflicts of interest, allocations), potential HMR&C matters and, possibly, concerns that investors are not being treated equally.

Electronic trading platforms

An integrated trading platform that permits automated trading or facilitates straight through processing is a powerful, efficient tool. Such a system generates significant cost savings and adds value, provided it has sufficient operational support. The degree to which prime brokers can offer these services varies, but those who do certainly give hedge funds a real "leg up".[1] Such a system not only helps a hedge fund gain good access to markets but it leads to greater efficiencies in execution and risk management.

It is essential when considering an integrated trading platform, or any software or back office platform, for the manager to bench test the product, negotiate the documentation carefully, ensure compatibility with current (and proposed) systems (both in-house and for interfaces with systems of other service providers), negotiate costs, consult with other service providers (in particular, the administrator and providers of risk management software) and obtain references from current users. Decisions should not be made based on presentation material, which quite often focuses on "bells and whistles", but on thorough due diligence. The directors of the hedge fund should have a demonstration, interview the purveyor and, in the proper discharge of their oversight responsibilities, have a say in cost and functionality issues. Hedge funds considering such a system should obtain examples of reports that the system generates (cash forecast ladders, FX exposures), speak to other funds that use the system to confirm reliability and the usefulness of the features that attracted the manager in the first place. One should examine carefully the calculations that the system is reputed to make for example, what are the parameters used in calculating BETA, can they be reconciled, how is credit and interest rate DV01 calculated, how are derivatives handled, etc. Whilst this can be a tedious process, it avoids the strains that may arise such as system breakdowns, incompatibility, less than promised functionality, errors and so on. A significant issue is the length of time required to implement updates or to fix problems. In such an event, if trades are DK'd or delays arise, it may not be possible to recover losses. Far worse is the spectre of having to trade round a platform with reduced functionality or to take it out completely.

Structured products

The topic of structured products raises may issues, economic and non-economic. It is the readiness or pro-activeness of the prime broker to offer to fund, structure or engage in this activity with the hedge fund that can further, or harm, the relationship. Some prime brokers perpetually offer structures to their hedge fund clients. Not all of these deals are appropriate, made at the right time or are cost effective. If they are done in the right way at the right time, they can provide a real benefit to the fund. Continuous dialogue and education helps to generate the flow of ideas, some of which might be quite useful. Quite often, total return swaps will enable hedge funds to gain economic exposures in companies where to acquire the equities would result in having to disclose holdings to the relevant authority. Similarly, using derivatives to avoid disclosure may result in other issues and might, in certain jurisdictions, kick off a disclosure obligation – such as in the UK where the Takeover Code now requires the disclosure of certain derivative positions in companies involved in take overs.

Another "structured product" that is gaining favour in the fixed income world is the extended repo facility. These enable the hedge fund to closely control their funding and leverage. Extended repo facilities are long dated repos where the essential terms are negotiated and agreed at the time of trade: liquidity; haircut rates; and other material terms. Some of these instruments can be extremely deep and have significant maturities. The beauty of these structures is that the hedge fund can manage its collateral on a portfolio basis, rather than managing a portfolio of repos. "Swapping" stocks in and out of such a structure may take place without having to worry about early calls or the risk of having to finance open positions. In general, such a facility is attractive where the hedge fund controls activity and the prime broker does not have the right to call an issue. It should be noted that this facility might be obtained not just from the prime broker, but also from other counterparties.

Tax efficient structures

The prime broker can play a pivotal role in the creation of tax efficient structures. Invariably, there is a wealth of expertise available in the prime broker and in its affiliates in the jurisdictions where the hedge fund trades. It is, however, axiomatic that different prime brokers have different areas of strength. The efficient execution of a deal quite often depends on local information and expertise. A prime broker who not only understands local requirements and idiosyncrasies, as well as the needs of the hedge fund, can bring added value – translated, often, into increased performance, lower costs and better fees.

Dividend enhancements

An example of a simple, effective tax efficient strategy is dividend enhancements. Essentially, the hedge fund lends its stock to a firm or institution in a local market for a defined period (usually when the stock goes ex-dividend) and receives a better tax treatment when the dividend is paid. Typically, the benefit is shared among the arranger, the fund and the borrower. These strategies have been around for a long time, but as tax regimes converge the benefit from such strategies may slowly decline.

Rehypothecation

Rehypothecation is an item that shapes the relationship but that is rarely discussed. For the prime broker, the assets in the portfolio that it holds and over which it has a security interest provide a readily available source of securities and other instruments that it may lend and for which it pays little or nothing and – for which it may earn a profit. The extent to which prime brokers can rehypothecate is dictated by legal requirements imposed on the prime broker, the PBA and the Offering Materials, and is influenced by lending rates, the quality of the portfolio, market conditions, the nature of the security interest over the portfolio and the liabilities of the hedge fund. In the US, there are rules governing the extent to which a prime broker can rehypothecate (140%, *see* related discussions in Chapters 2 and 3). In Europe there is no such limit, and the range can be anywhere from 100% to full access to the long side of the book. The appetite of the directors to permit a prime broker to leverage the portfolio solely to its pecuniary advantage tempers hypothecation. Directors may wish to impose limits on prime broker hypothecation but doing so in an aggressive manner might result in higher fees or other "roadblocks" being activated or implemented.

Concerns about hypothecation do arise when the prime broker hypothecates uncharged positions, where cash is returned to the portfolio rather than "equivalent securities" and when the directors challenge the profits made by the prime broker as excessive. Rehypothecation increases the hedge funds exposure to the prime broker. It is when these issues arise or when the hedge fund experiences distress that the real impact is felt. Thus, there must be a constant dialogue among the manager, directors and prime broker to ensure that all aspects of hypothecation are understood, that clear provisions to govern this are in place and that if the directors require changes, they may be implemented with minimum fuss and expense.

PRIME BROKERAGE COSTS

The relationship with the prime broker is robust and delicate. The question of costs is always a subject of discussion and, unless controlled, a point of contention. The query is whether the costs should be "what we should actually pay" or be the subject of a "cost cutting" exercise. Looking at the bottom line figure can give a hedge fund comfort, but it can also give a hedge fund cause for concern. While using a prime broker yields operational efficiencies that outweigh the costs of unbundled prime brokerage services, a thorough analysis can reveal the true costs a hedge fund pays. One must measure, for example, the costs of dealing away and give-ups against the achieved price for dealing solely through the prime broker, or the costs of the manager handling it own borrowing and lending. An obvious candidate would be the rates achieved on foreign exchange transactions achieved by dealing away, eg, FX trading.

Single *vs* multiple prime brokers

In the early stages of a hedge fund's life there is a need to achieve simplicity and one stop shopping. A prime broker, as we have seen, can offer multiple services, all of which contribute to enhanced, cost effective services and a successful relationship. As hedge funds grow, they achieve growth and stature, become sophisticated in both trading and portfolio composition, require increasingly sophisticated tools to trade and measure risk and performance, but need to control costs. It is at this point that a review of the services offered by prime brokers takes place, whether or not at the request of the directors, and when it might be found that these may be impediments to growth, flexibility and other considerations. Adding a second prime broker at this time, or even earlier, can give the hedge fund flexibility in achieving its needs but also a degree of leverage in terms of their relationship with their prime brokers. It may also achieve the need of giving the hedge fund a prime broker in a geographical or product market into which the hedge fund wishes to enter. To the prime broker, the risk of losing a client and associated revenue can sometimes lead to increased "flexibility" which may translate into better services and lower costs.

Funds with large AUMs seek to diversify their counterparty risk. Global hedge funds seek to gain the best access to their target markets. Having multiple prime brokers may help the hedge fund achieve its goals. It is wise to maximise all of the means at one's disposal to achieve efficient trading, maximise returns and control costs.

There are, however, downsides to having multiple prime brokers. One potential downside of running multiple prime brokers arises from having a fund's positions distributed around the market, which may make risk control and consolidation difficult if the wrong systems and processes are not in place.

LEVERAGE

One of the most essential tools available to a hedge fund is the ability to leverage. Leverage can be achieved in many ways. Leverage involves the borrowing of funds and the investing of those borrowed funds in other assets. The borrowing is usually collateralised over existing assets. The new assets, in turn, may be used to raise more cash that, in turn, may be used to purchase more assets. In theory, but not in practice, this can go on *ad infinitum*. The counterparty providing the lending will without exception impose a haircut and lend less than the present value of the collateral, and levy a charge in the process. The inherent inefficiencies limit the absolute number of times that the hedge fund can repeat this trade.[2]

One of the essentials of any prime brokerage service is providing leverage. This has long been the norm in the equity long/short world, and is a feature of fixed income funds. Traditionally, fixed income funds have looked to the highly efficient repo market (not necessarily facing the prime broker) to secure their leverage as opposed to long-short equity hedge funds who source leverage from their prime broker.

The advantage of using the prime broker is that it can significantly reduce operational overhead. There is a cost of this, however, and that is the ceding of control over the portfolio. Letting the prime broker source leverage may put the hedge fund in a more exposed position in respect to credit exposure. Often, PBAs do not afford as much protection to the fund's assets as would, eg, a GRMA when executed with a third party.

INTERMEDIATION

Potentially one of the most time consuming and heavily resourced activities at a hedge fund (alone or with an administrator) can be the confirmation and settlement of derivatives, especially CDSs. (A CDS may be likened to the buying or selling of protection/insurance on the credit worthiness of an issuer.) While the market has moved a long way towards standardisation, there are still many issues to be resolved, particularly if a hedge fund has several ISDA counterparties. The use of multiple counterparties can also lead to inefficient uses of capital since invariably each transaction will have some form of collateralisation. Conversely, there may be benefits where there are numerous transactions that, if netted, might well lead to some benefits in the form of reduced costs.

Within a single counterparty, if the hedge fund has a soundly negotiated, balanced ISDA, one may expect to use cross product netting (where collateral requirements form long and short obligations can be offset).

If derivatives are to be used, effective ISDA negotiation should be a priority. Hedge funds, especially young/small funds, will accept terms offered to them in an effort to secure a relationship and achieve the ability to transact with a particular counterparty – dealing outweighs negotiation. In such a case, the new hedge fund is subject to provisions that are not within the market standards for large, mature hedge funds. Such terms, including NAV decline triggers, key man losses, late delivery of documents, and so on, as additional termination events, low additional cross termination amounts and onerous events of default, leaves a new fund in a precarious position should anything go wrong – including market declines, large redemptions and so on. Promises to renegotiate terms in such instances or to forego exercising provisions are more often than not reduced to writing.

There are ways in which this can be avoided. The first is to negotiate to achieve the same terms across all counterparties. This can be a timely and costly process. However, balancing this is the spectre of uneven ISDA provisions that increases operational and credit risk. Alternatively, a hedge fund can look to intermediation. Intermediation is essentially a "give-up agreement" where the hedge fund can deal with any counterparty with whom it has an ISDA in place, which trade is then given up to the prime broker so that the fund is left facing the prime broker. This introduces increased credit exposure to the prime broker, but at the same time the hedge fund benefits from reduced collateralisation due to the netting of trades. The overhead is further reduced since in executing the intermediation the prime broker will undoubtedly employ the checks and balances that would be left with the hedge fund if it maintained its deals with their trade counterparts.

It should be noted that it is still essential to have and to trade under ISDAs in place with the hedge fund's other counterparties. In this case, existence of cross default clauses and NAV decline triggers, unequal or evened out across the hedge fund's documentation, can still put the fund in a position of "discomfort".

The introduction of intermediation has meant a great deal to many hedge funds, simplifying their derivative (especially CDS) trading activity and helping control costs. Prime brokers have also benefited due to increased revenues. Offering an integrated trading platform at an early stage helps not only to ensure continued trade flow and activity but also to recoup costs.

CONCLUSION

Prime brokerage allows hedge funds to maximise their credit relationships and activities while improving efficiency. In addition, prime brokerage streamlines the credit and documentation process, given that the hedge fund is subject to one internal credit review and executes one master trading agreement and credit support annex with the prime broker, rather than many agreements with multiple dealers. An effective PBA provides for the more efficient use of collateral for margin relationships. Margin positions can be netted as the hedge fund needs to manage one credit relationship to achieve trading relationships with many counterparties. In addition, the client is able to access pricing and liquidity from a greater number of dealers and potentially to expand the range of its activities.

There are many factors that drive the hedge fund–prime broker relationship. Many are positive, but negative experiences leave a lasting taint on the relationship and may even serve to dissuade new hedge funds from using a particular prime broker. What are the avoidable issues? Promises to renegotiate or to forebear using clauses that are postponed. Promises to introduce prospects that lead to little or no investment. Automated systems that do not operate, that do not provide promised or required functionality or that are not bug-free. Hastily withdrawn, or no, seed capital. DK'd trades or misbookings. Non-payment of interest on balances, over-collateralisation of derivative and FX transactions, unilateral amendments to PBAs or other documents without providing the appropriate or advance notification. Overcharging, dramatically increased fees or a lack of transparency in charging. A reluctance to process give-ups. Fails to deliver when there is inventory.

Quite often it falls on the administrator to address and rectify the problems, but serious issues require the attention of the individual fund managers in the manager itself, or even the directors. This saps resources and undoubtedly affects performance.

Ultimately, and for final consideration, is the query whether it really matters how much a hedge fund pays a prime broker, as long as the hedge fund receives good performance, the NAV per share increases and investors and service providers are happy. Happiness and indifference to fees do not always go hand in hand. Costs and fees, key planks in the economic fabric of the hedge fund–prime broker relationship, will always play a part and will have an impact on the hedge fund's trading. Ultimately, the goals of every investor, and of the hedge fund, the prime broker and the directors, are to limit exposure and risk, to make money and to keep expenses under control. These in turn lead to sound economics and a healthy trading relationship. Achieve a healthy balance and all parties involved realise a win-win. Lose the balance and the relationship may become soured, or fall apart. In the end, as there will always be hedge funds and prime brokers, there will always be trading and economics to help share this relationship – for the sake of the markets and investors, for the better.

---

1   *See* "Citigroup unveils new prime brokerage platform", MarketWatch Weekend Edition, Dow Jones, 2 August 2006, available at www.marketwatch.com/News/Story/ 9CrbKW296mFr9n8npZ5BxNg?siteid=mktw&dist=TNMostMailed

2   For example, a fund holding €1 borrows €1, giving it €2 to invest. If the investment pays off, the fund's €2 would become €4 that, after the repayment of the €1 loan would leave the fund with €3 and a return of 200%, *vs* 100% if the fund did not borrow (or leverage) with its original €1. The risk, of course, is that the markets turn against the fund and the €2 investment shrinks to, say, 50 cents. You then can cash out at 50 cents, but have to repay the €1 borrowed, leaving the fund with nothing or, if the decline is severe or the leverage is great, a loss.

7

Corporate Governance by and for Hedge Funds

Barry P. Barbash

Willkie Farr & Gallagher LLP

INTRODUCTION

The phrase "corporate governance" has traditionally not been associated with the operation of hedge funds; indeed hedge fund governance could long have been seen as an oxymoron. Hedge funds throughout the world today, however, increasingly appear to be assuming the role of corporate activists with respect to the companies in which they invest, with the aim of "unlocking" value in those companies and making known their views on typical governance issues such as poison pills, composition of a board of directors and executive compensation. Capitalising on this trend, some hedge funds operate as "governance funds," whose primary investment objectives contemplate regularly engaging in these activities.[1]

Hedge fund governance today is far from one-directional. Funds are not only increasingly concerned with the structure and operation of their portfolio companies, but have also become subject to greater pressure to enhance their own structure and operations. Public and private employee benefits plans and other institutional investors, which have all become key investors in hedge funds, have assumed an active role in drafting the terms and conditions to which hedge funds are subject.[2] In addition, a recent trend towards

The author would like to acknowledge the assistance of Willkie Farr & Gallagher LLP associates Jennifer R. Suellentrop, Michael Ponder and Eric C. Goldstein, in preparing this chapter.

greater regulation of hedge funds – most notably illustrated by the implementation by the SEC's adoption of Advisers Act Rule 203(b)(3)-2 has resulted in a far greater number of obligations being placed on a wide range of hedge fund activities.[3]

This chapter describes the two sides of hedge fund governance. The first part of this chapter discusses hedge funds as corporate activists, the "new sheriffs of [the] boardroom," as they were called recently,[4] and looks at the various ways in which funds implement programs of governance in attempting to realise shareholder value. The second part of this chapter describes how market and regulatory pressures are, in essence, requiring successful hedge funds to become more disciplined and formalise their own governance structures. "Corporate governance" or "governance" as used in this chapter refers to the various aspects of the structure or operation of an entity (portfolio company or hedge fund) that support or define the relationship among all of those parties participating in the entity (eg, management, board of directors and shareholders, general partner, and limited partners).

Hedge funds as corporate activists

A word of caution

Unlike mutual funds and other investment companies subject to extensive regulation, hedge funds historically have not been required to file detailed reports of their operations with government regulators. As a result, assessing past trends or activities of hedge funds can be quite difficult and subject to a fair degree of imprecision. The discussion in this chapter is based on press accounts, book and other published materials on hedge funds, as well as on the author's experiences as a practitioner advising numerous hedge fund clients.

Historical passivity in investments

Hedge funds have historically followed the traditional "Wall Street rule" and "voted with their feet"; if a fund manager believed that a portfolio company was underperforming, the manager would simply sell the fund's shares in the company.[5] Most hedge funds appear to continue to follow the same rule today, despite recent press coverage that suggests that many hedge funds have become corporate activists.[6]

That hedge funds have not played an active role in the affairs of their portfolio companies does not seem surprising in light of the way many, if not most, fund managers have in the past overseen their funds' investments. Hedge fund managers have historically managed their funds so as to take advantage of relatively small movements in the markets. Such an objective is often facilitated by relatively rapid buying and selling of investments and spreading a fund's assets over a large number of investments. Rapid turnover and small investment positions are generally inconsistent with the long-term commitment and substantial holdings usually required to enable an investment manager to become an activist seeking change in the structure and operations of a portfolio company.

Growth in hedge fund corporate activism
Private equity and venture capital funds have long taken an active role in the affairs of their portfolio companies. Venture capital funds have often purchased the securities of companies experiencing financial distress and have sought to profit from those companies' weaknesses by seeking either to transform them into viable marketplace participants or to find profitable methods to dissolve them and gain a return on their investments. Private equity funds have often sought to couple their investments in companies whose securities are not public with participation in the management of those companies in an effort to prevent those investments from experiencing significant dilution or other adverse consequences. Over the last few years, however, a new and noticeable trend has begun: a number of hedge funds and other private investment funds have adopted investment strategies that in many fundamental ways resemble the business practices of venture capital and private equity funds.

The law underlying hedge fund activism
Hedge funds are formed under the laws of countries throughout the world and invest in the securities of companies organised in a host of jurisdictions. The significant number of countries to whose laws hedge funds are subject makes it difficult, if not impracticable, to catalogue the laws governing hedge funds' involvement with the operations of their portfolio companies. None the less, some generalisations, drawn principally from the laws of the US and the Cayman Islands, which tend to be more developed than those of

some other popular jurisdictions for hedge fund formation, can be made and are summarised below.

Does an obligation to engage in activism exist?
A critical question for every hedge fund manager is whether the manager is required under applicable law to undertake any action with respect to companies whose securities are held by that manager's fund. No court or securities regulator in any jurisdiction appears to have answered that question. Application of legal principles identified as generally governing the conduct of money managers that, like hedge fund managers, have discretion to make investments on behalf of others, would seem to lead to the conclusion that hedge fund managers could, at least under some circumstances, be required to take action with respect to portfolio companies.

In the US typical hedge fund manager, by virtue of the control it exerts over the investments of its fund, would be deemed a "fiduciary" with respect to the fund.[7] Managers in other jurisdiction, including the UK, France and Japan, also owe jiduciary duties to their clients. As a fiduciary, the manager is subject to various obligations, including an affirmative duty to act in the best interests of its client[8] – the fund – and to seek to achieve the fund's investment objective.[9] The objective of many, if not most, hedge funds is high absolute returns. Achieving those returns may necessitate the fund's manager, or board of directors, taking action with respect to the fund's portfolio companies. Whether such action must be taken depends on an analysis of the costs of and benefits to the fund.[10] If the benefits clearly outweigh the costs, then action should be taken.[11]

Limitations and/or disclosure as to the nature of
investment positions
Fulfilling its fiduciary obligations when engaging in governance activities involving portfolio companies is only the starting point for a hedge fund manager. Equally important for the activist manager are specific laws and rules that govern the purchase and sale of certain types of securities. One such provision of consequence is Regulation 13D-G under the Exchange Act often referred to as the SEC's "beneficial ownership" rule.

The beneficial ownership rule generally requires any person who becomes the beneficial owner of more than 5% of any class of voting equity securities registered under the Exchange Act to file a report with various entities, including the SEC. Beneficial ownership is measured by voting and investment power with respect to the securities in question. The classes of equity securities registered under the Exchange Act include stocks, warrants and convertible debt securities that are listed on a US national securities exchange (today this includes NASDAQ) and some that are quoted in the "pink sheets". The beneficial ownership rule can apply to both a hedge fund and the fund's manager. The report required to be filed under the rule must contain specified information, including the extent of the reporting person's position in the securities.

Under the beneficial ownership rule, a hedge fund manager and/or the hedge fund itself is required to report all positions meeting the rule's 5% threshold. In some instances, the report needs to be made on the SEC's Schedule 13D under the Exchange Act. If a hedge fund is a "Qualified Institutional Investor" and a "Passive Investor" as defined in the beneficial ownership rule, it is permitted to file on Schedule 13G, an abbreviated form, so long as the securities being reported were acquired in the ordinary course of the filer's business and "not with the purpose nor with the effect of changing or influencing control of the issuer". A passive investor may not file a Schedule 13G if it directly or indirectly beneficially owns 20% or more of the issuer. The term qualified institutional investor includes brokers, dealers and registered (US federal or state) investment advisers. A hedge fund manager and/or hedge fund that desires to take a major corporate action with respect to a portfolio company would likely not be eligible to file a Schedule 13G.

Communicating with other investors

A hedge fund may often hold an equity interest in a portfolio company that is substantial, but not sufficient by itself to influence the portfolio company's management or business plan. In such a case, the fund's manager may seek to cause the fund to pursue a proxy contest as a means to exert control over the portfolio company.[12] When pursuing a proxy contest, the fund will need to meet specialised rules applicable to such a contest, including the proxy solicitation rules adopted by the SEC under Section 14 of the Exchange Act. These rules limit the ability of a shareholder of a portfolio company, including a hedge fund, to communicate with other investors. The rules also limit how a hedge fund can present shareholder proposals on various topics for a vote on the portfolio company's proxy statement.

Rules against misuse of inside information

Many jurisdictions throughout the world have adopted provisions prohibiting market participants, such as hedge funds, from trading on the basis of significant information relating to a publicly-traded company that has not been publicly disseminated.[13] Such prohibited trading is often referred to as trading on "inside information". In recent years, a number of hedge fund managers have been found to have violated these sorts of provisions in the United States.[14]

A hedge fund manager registered under the Advisers Act is subject not only to general prohibitions on trading on inside information, but also to a requirement to establish and maintain procedures designed reasonably to prevent the misuse of such information. A registered hedge fund manager often includes such procedures in a code of ethics to which the manager's employees are subject.

Becoming an insider

An activist manager of a hedge fund that invests substantially in the securities of a portfolio company could become an "insider" of the company precluded from certain trading in the company's securities. Under Section 16 of the Exchange Act a hedge fund with a substantial holding in a portfolio company cannot engage in short-term trading (the section contemplates a time period of six months) of the company's securities.[15] The section would also require a representative of an activist hedge fund that became an officer or director of the portfolio company to file reports in connection with certain purchases and sales of the portfolio company's securities. Section 16 also generally precludes an insider from engaging in short sales of the securities of an issuer.

Other trading and market rules

Managers of activist hedge funds need to be aware of other rules affecting trading in new issues and other securities. Regulation M under the Exchange Act, generally prohibits distribution participants (including "affiliated purchasers," a term that can encompass investment advisers, including those to hedge funds) from purchasing or bidding for certain securities during an offering. The NASD has proposed rules pertaining to sales by NASD member broker–dealer firms to investors, including hedge funds that explicitly or implicitly agree to compensate the broker–dealer with trades at inflated commission rates. Hedge fund managers should also be aware of NASD Rule 2790 that restrict sales of new issues like initial public offerings to certain portfolio managers that may be hedge fund managers and owners of broker–dealers.

Takeover rules

Hedge funds that seek to participate in an acquisition of a portfolio company should be aware of anti-takeover and related rules that have been enacted by many jurisdictions. Under US securities laws a hedge fund would be prohibited from making a tender offer for Exchange Act-registered equity securities if success in the offer would result in the hedge funds owning more than 5% of the class of equity securities, unless any required filings are made.[16] Under the Exchange Act, a hedge fund is also precluded from making any untrue statement of a material fact or omitting to state any material fact necessary in order to make the statements made, in the light of the circumstances under which they are made, not misleading, or to engage in any fraudulent, deceptive, or manipulative acts or practices, in connection with any tender offer or request or invitation for tenders, or any solicitation of security holders in opposition to or in favour of any such offer, request, or invitation.[17] Such a hedge fund may also become subject to statutes adopted by a significant number of states in the US that regulate takeovers.[18] A hedge fund may also be subject to the notification and pre-clearance requirements imposed by the US Hart Scott Rodino Act, a statute intended to address anti-competitive acquisitions, but which is broad enough to apply to the acquisition of substantial blocks of securities of an issuer by a hedge fund.

Poison pill provisions

Anti-takeover tactics such as the "poison pill" can present concerns for hedge funds that wish to gain control of a portfolio company.

Under a typical poison pill strategy, the acquisition by a hedge fund of more than 10% of such a company would trigger an automatic discount share offer to all existing shareholders of the company other than the acquirer, diluting the percentage of the company owned by the acquiring hedge fund and making it more expensive for the hedge fund to acquire the company's stock. In efforts to avoid poison pills, hedge funds recently have teamed up to gain control collectively of target companies. In response, target companies have developed new anti-takeover tactics, such as allowing their largest creditors to demand immediate payment in the event of a takeover, barring investors with significant holdings in the company from serving on the company's board, and avoiding the election of new directors by not holding an annual meeting.

How hedge fund corporate activism works

Recent activism by hedge funds throughout the world has taken various forms. Some hedge fund managers have been reported as designating a portion of their funds for private equity or venture capital-like investments in an effort to obtain high absolute returns in an environment in which achieving those returns is increasingly difficult.[19] Other hedge fund managers seeking those kinds of returns have caused their funds to invest in the securities of a small number of companies.[20] The small number of investments, in turn, has often led to a manager having significant in-depth knowledge of portfolio companies and/or substantial investment positions in those companies. Significant knowledge and concentrated investment position are key elements in providing hedge fund managers with the ability to influence the operations of portfolio companies. Types of activism in which hedge funds have engaged over the recent past have included seeking to: change management of portfolio companies through publicity; put pressure on or undertake collaborative discussions with management; elect alternate slates of directors of portfolio companies with the intention of moulding board actions or decision-making; or effect changes in control of portfolio companies.[21] Hedge fund managers have also used proxy contests to influence the policies and management of portfolio companies.

Some corporate actions by hedge funds have been particularly bold. Hedge funds, for instance, recently sought to oust management of

Germany's principal stock market and gain control of the London Stock Exchange.[22]

Practical problems arising from active involvement in the affairs of portfolio companies

Those hedge funds that have become active over the recent past in the affairs of their portfolio companies appear to have experienced mixed results. Some of the practical problems that those funds and their managers have reportedly faced are described below.

Conflicts with other investors

Hedge fund managers have found their actions and interests in conflict with those of other institutional investors as they have become more aggressive in their willingness to challenge managements of their funds' portfolio companies and have sought to cause substantive changes in the operation and structure of those companies. Principal among the investors in disagreement with hedge fund managers' tactics are employee benefit plan managers. At the root of the conflict between activist hedge funds and employee benefit plan managers would appear to be different investment horizons. A manager of a typical defined benefit plan invests for the longer-term, which can often be ten or more years, whereas a typical hedge fund often invests for a far shorter period. Many employee benefit plan managers have worried that the managers of hedge funds that engage in active corporate restructuring of, or seek to change, portfolio companies' boards or management focus only on maximising short-term profitability of the investments and not the long-term success of those companies.[23] Managers of union pension plans have also expressed concerns that many of the suggestions hedge fund managers make to public company management can often lead to an overall downsizing of the portfolio companies and to lost jobs, a result that is viewed by representatives of organised labour as contrary to the unions that are sponsors of those plans.[24] Hedge funds' positions regarding the proposed structure and organisation of many public companies also complicate the tension and unease between the goals of hedge funds and their managers and the policy objectives of many employee benefit plans also invested in hedge funds.

Governance within hedge funds

As discussed later in this chapter, hedge funds, wherever formed, are typically structured to offer the maximum investment flexibility to their decision-making bodies, the managing member, in the case of a limited liability company, the general partner in the case of a limited partnership, or the board of directors in the case of a company or corporation. The desire to achieve investment flexibility has historically caused hedge fund managers not to focus their efforts on internal fund governance matters.

Corporate governance as an afterthought

The traditional picture of a hedge fund manager is that of an entrepreneur seeking to escape the bureaucratic world of large financial services firms and wanting to invest subject to the fewest restrictions and rules. The traditional investor in a hedge fund is a high net worth individual seeking high absolute returns. The combination of the traditional hedge fund manager and hedge fund client has resulted in hedge funds operating subject to only minimal restrictions on their structure and operations. As one commenter has said "Governance in the hedge fund world has been something of an afterthought, addressed primarily for due-diligence purposes. Governance is rarely formally codified in fund documentation or treated as an indispensable factor for a fund's success."[25] That afterthought nature of hedge fund governance is often reflected by many actions, policies and procedures of hedge funds being left to the "discretion" or the "sole discretion" of hedge fund managers. The lack of emphasis on fund governance is often reflected in the delegation to the investment managers of hedge funds formed under the laws of the Cayman Islands, an often preferred jurisdiction for non-US hedge funds, of most of a fund's formal oversight, with limited oversight duties given to the boards of directors of those funds.

Over the past few years, the idea of governance as an afterthought for hedge funds and their managers has begun to be replaced by the notion of governance as potentially significant to the success of hedge funds. The sources of the trend towards a greater focus on hedge fund governance appear to be a new breed of hedge fund investors and an increase in the amount of governmental regulation to which hedge fund managers are now, or will be in the future, subject.

Demands of institutional investors

The traditional high net worth individual investors in hedge funds have been joined recently by a new breed of fund investors, institutional investors such as public and private employee benefit plans, foundations, college endowments and funds of funds, all of which appear to be increasingly investing in hedge funds. Among these institutional investors, employee benefit plans seem to have increased their hedge fund investments by the greatest amounts. According to a relatively recent press account, by 2008 these plans may invest almost US$300 billion in hedge funds.[26] Although plan investments in hedge funds represent only a small percentage of aggregate hedge fund assets under management, the rate by which plans are investing in hedge funds is growing exponentially,[27] according to William H. Donaldson, former Chairman of the SEC.

A second category of institutional investors investing in hedge funds of greater prominence in recent years are funds of funds.[28] As their name implies, funds of funds are investment pools that themselves invest in interests of hedge funds. Funds of funds typically market themselves as offering prospective investors the benefits of diversified portfolios of hedge fund investments, and generally undertake, on their investors' behalf, due diligence of the managers of the hedge funds whose interests the funds of funds hold.

Employee benefit plans and funds of funds have been in the forefront of the efforts of hedge fund investors to become more active in the structure and operations of hedge funds. Two principal reasons seem to account for those efforts. Managers of both employee benefit plans and hedge funds are themselves fiduciaries with respect to the monies they invest; seeking to meet those fiduciary duties may cause the managers both to conduct more rigorous due diligence efforts than traditional individual hedge fund investors and to participate more actively than those investors in setting the terms and conditions to be met. Employee benefit plan and funds of funds managers are also subject to substantive legal requirements that can necessitate hedge funds, in which interest employee benefit plans or funds of funds invest, agreeing to operate in a particular manner.

Specific terms and conditions sought by institutional investors
Activist hedge fund investors seek a wide variety of governance features and/or provisions to be added to the partnership or corporate documents under which they typically operate. A sample of some of the more prevalent provisions currently being added include those described below.

Independent directors
The advisers/sponsors of many hedge funds formed outside the US operate subject to oversight by boards of directors who are independent of the advisers/sponsors. These directors typically review the overall business and performance of their funds and deal with issues that fall outside the funds' operating guidelines, such as approving special arrangements with key investors relating to liquidity or fees. The directors may also be charged with responsibility for reviewing and approving transactions between advisers/sponsors and their funds, presenting conflicts of interest.[29]

Hedge funds that choose to list their shares for trading on an exchange are often required to have directors independent of their managers. Institutional investors increasingly appear to seek to have hedge funds in which they invest appoint independent directors. Such directors are often employees or officers of service providers of the funds such as administrators or custodians.

Provisions on valuation of investments
Valuation by hedge funds of investments, such as thinly traded or illiquid investments, continues to be an important topic for hedge fund institutional investors. Such investors appear to be concerned about the conflict of interest presented when the manager (or General Partner) of a hedge fund has responsibility for such valuation; the manager (or General Partner) has an incentive in such a case to use higher valuations so as to earn a higher performance fee. In attempting to deal with the conflict, institutional investors may require hedge fund managers to document valuations, to use independent pricing services in calculating the valuation of some or all securities held by hedge funds and to implement committee structures to handle pricing.

Limitations on the use of side pockets

Many hedge fund managers retain the power to designate certain illiquid investments held by their funds as appropriate for placement in "side pockets" for purposes of valuation. Such an investment is not valued for purposes of calculating the fund's net asset value until the investment can be valued and/or redeemed.

A side pocket, which is generally used to benefit the interest of a hedge fund's investors, can subject the fund's manager to a conflict; the manager may have the incentive to use a side pocket to increase the fund's performance. In an effort to reduce the potential for such a conflict, the investors in a hedge fund often seek provisions limiting the use of side pockets. Limitations vary from allowing such use only if objective criteria are met to establishing specific periods of time over which side pockets can be employed. Investors may also require that investments held in side pockets be valued upon specified withdrawals of capital being made from the fund.

Limitations on the use of side letters

The practice of some hedge fund managers of entering into so-called "side letters" with select investors in funds has come to be seen by some institutional investors as potentially resulting in inappropriate disparate treatment of investors. Exchanges where shares of hedge funds are listed consider this not to be equal treatment of investors institutional investors often try to prevent this result by negotiating terms and conditions with a fund manager restricting the use of side letters by requiring written explanations for the entering into of side letters. In such a letter, a manager of a hedge fund may agree with one or more of the fund's investors to agree to "key man" provisions, favourable management fees for the investors, "high water" marks, lock-up provisions and withdrawal terms, increased reporting of portfolio securities and disclosure of material compliance events/investigations by a regulatory authority.

Audit issues

Not all hedge funds are not at present generally subject to any statutory or regulatory requirement to audit their financial statements. In a typical case, a fund's operating documents will set out whether an audit of the fund will be performed and whether the fund's investors will receive the audited financial statements.

(Exchange-listed hedge funds do have this requirement.) Hedge fund institutional investors increasingly are mandating that their funds hire independent accounting firms to conduct audits and make those audits available to all investors in the funds. Some hedge funds have also been required to form audit committees to oversee the conducting and reporting of audits.

Periodic performance reports

Institutional hedge fund investors appear to becoming bolder in requesting more information from the hedge funds in which they invest. Services designed to standardise such information have also become operational in the recent past.

Governance as a by-product of increased regulation

Most, if not all, hedge fund managers have historically had as a central business goal investing the monies of their funds outside of the scope of the greatest amount of regulation feasible. This goal has become increasingly difficult to achieve in recent years, as regulators throughout the world have sought to keep up with the substantial growth in aggregate hedge fund assets under management.

Clearly the most significant of recent regulatory initiatives affecting hedge funds is Rule 203(b)(3)-2 adopted by the SEC in 2004 effective in February 2006.[30] The rule narrowed the scope of an exclusion from the definition of an investment adviser set out in the Advisers Act on which hedge fund managers have in the past generally relied in operating outside of the provisions of the Advisers Act.[31] The intended effect of the rule was to require many, if not most, hedge fund managers to register as investment advisers under the Advisers Act and to become subject to the Act's various substantive provisions.

When it adopted the hedge fund manager registration rule, the SEC maintained that the rule was not intended to restrict the investment opportunities of hedge funds. The SEC's assertion will would have proved to be correct with respect to hedge fund investments if the Rule has not been vacated. Other aspects of the operations of hedge funds, however, are likely to be significantly affected by the application of the Advisers Act and its rule to hedge fund managers that register.[32] Many of these provisions can be seen to impose governance measures and may serve as models for regulators in jurisdictions outside the US. Some of the more significant provisions are summarised overleaf.

Compliance policies

A hedge fund manager registered as an investment adviser needs to adopt policies and procedures that are "reasonably designed" to prevent violation of the Advisers Act and rules promulgated thereunder".[33] These policies and procedures must be reviewed annually for adequacy and effectiveness. The same rule will require that managers appoint a chief compliance officer, whose role is to administer the managers' compliance policies and procedures.[34] The practical effect of the provisions of the rule will be to necessitate a hedge fund manager's not only adopting written compliance policies and procedures, but also establishing and maintaining an effective means to implement them. Neither the SEC nor its staff have to date set out a list of all matters that a hedge fund manager's compliance program must address. The SEC has, however, expressed the expectation that a compliance program should cover, to the extent applicable, at least the following topics:

❏ the processes used in managing clients' investments including processes designed to ensure that: (a) investment opportunities are allocated among clients; (b) portfolios of clients are maintained consistent with the clients' investment objectives; (c) necessary disclosures are made by the manager; and (d) applicable regulatory restrictions are met by the manager's personnel;
❏ trading practices, on behalf of clients, including: (a) procedures implemented to satisfy the manager's "best execution" obligations; (b) policies followed by the manager in using client brokerage to obtain research and other services; and (c) procedures used to govern aggregated trade allocation;
❏ the manager's proprietary trading practices and procedures, as well as those covering the personal trading activities of the manager's personnel;
❏ the accuracy of disclosures made by the manager;
❏ procedures implemented by the manager to safeguard client assets from conversion or inappropriate use by the manager's personnel;

❑ the accurate creation of records required under the Advisers Act and their maintenance;

❑ policies and procedures applied to marketing of the manager's services, including the use of solicitors;

❑ processes used to value client holdings and assess fees on the basis of those valuations;

❑ the adoption of safeguards for the privacy protection of client records and information; and

❑ business continuity plans established by the manager.

The SEC has acknowledged that hedge fund managers may need to tailor their compliance policies and procedures to their funds' operations. The SEC has cited allocation of investment opportunities and trade aggregation as examples of areas that may necessitate such tailored policies and procedures. The SEC has advised hedge fund managers in connection with compliance measures "to ensure that their personnel are cognizant of and comply with the rules and regulations applicable to their business operations including compliance with rules and regulations applicable to private offerings and sales practices, anti-money laundering, soft dollar practices, insider trading and market manipulation and policies and procedures on disclosure, custody controls, cash solicitation procedures, disciplinary and financial condition disclosure and proxy voting, as well as potential examination by the SEC."[35]

Codes of ethics

Under an Advisers Act rule, a registered hedge fund manager needs to adopt a code of ethics that governs trading by the personnel of the manager who come within the definition of "access person" set out in the rule.[36] The code also needs to describe the compliance procedures to be used in overseeing the trading and address the manager's use of material, non-public information and establish a standard of business conduct applicable to the manager's employees.

Self-custody

An Advisers Act rule related to custody of client assets for registered investment advisers may be applicable to hedge fund managers that are registered as investment advisers and meet the broad definition of custody in the rule.[37] Hedge fund managers subject to the custody rule must use designated entities as custodians for their assets and meet certain other requirements. Many registered hedge fund advisers rely on an exemption in the rule that effectively requires their funds to have independent audits conducted and deliver annual audited financial statements to investors in the funds within a specified period of time.

Solicitation activities

A registered hedge fund manager is subject to limitations on the activities on third parties that solicit investors for the fund.[38] The application of the rule can have the practical effect of making the offer and sale of interest in the fund more difficult.

Advertising

A registered hedge fund manager must operate in accordance with a number of specific rules governing advertisements of the fund's performance.[39] The term "advertisement" is defined very broadly for this purpose and can include much of the correspondence a hedge fund manager provides to the fund's investors. Under the rule, a manager is precluded from using any advertisement that contains any untrue statement of a material fact or that is otherwise false or misleading. The rule also precludes a number of specified practices.

Advisory agreement provisions

An advisory agreement between a hedge fund manager that is a registered investment adviser and its client – the fund – is required to contain certain provisions, including most importantly that no assignment of the agreement can be made without the client's consent. Under the Advisers Act, "assignment" is defined to cover a case in which the adviser is acquired by another company notwithstanding that the personnel serving the client remain the same after the acquisition closes.[40] The effect of complying with the Advisers Act advisory agreement provisions is to set a governance standard applicable to a change of control of a hedge fund's manager.

Principal transactions

Under the Advisers Act, a principal securities transaction between an investment adviser of a hedge fund and the fund cannot be undertaken without the adviser providing notice to, and obtaining consent from, the fund.[41] Many hedge fund managers engage in principal transactions with their funds. The practical results of the notice and consent requirements is to regulate the process by which a manager can buy securities from or sell securities to the fund as principal.

Proxy voting

The SEC has taken the position that registered advisers given the power to vote proxies on behalf of their advisory clients have a fiduciary duty to vote proxies in the best interests of those clients.[42] An SEC rule requires a registered investment adviser to adopt policies and procedures that: (a) must specify how the adviser will address material conflicts that may arise between the interests of the adviser and its clients in connection with the voting of proxies; (b) disclose how clients can learn how the adviser voted proxies; and (c) describe the advisers specific proxy voting policies and procedures and make them available, upon request.[43] The need for a hedge fund manager to comply with this rule will likely result in the manager's adopting a degree of formality in voting proxies not typical of hedge funds generally to date.

Fiduciary obligations

The SEC has articulated the view that a hedge fund manager registered under the Adviser Act is a fiduciary with respect to the fund and is subject to the same obligations imposed generally on Advisers Act registrants. Over time, the SEC has identified a number of specific obligations arising from a registered adviser's fiduciary status, including:

❏ the duty to make full and fair disclosure to clients of all facts material to their continued use of the manager;
❏ the duty to have a reasonable, independent basis for its investment advice;
❏ the duty to obtain best execution for its clients' securities transactions where the adviser is in a position to direct brokerage transactions;
❏ the duty to ensure that the investment advice provided to a client is suitable for the client's objectives, needs and circumstances;

❑ the duty to refrain from effecting personal securities transactions inconsistent with client interests; and

❑ the duty to be loyal to clients.

The SEC staff has also cited the fiduciary status of a registered investment adviser in effectively setting procedural standards for such an adviser when engaging in various conduct. The staff is of the view, that a registered adviser, in handling an error in the undertaking of clients' securities transactions, cannot use brokerage commissions incurred on behalf of clients to compensate brokers for trade errors or have the account of one client absorb such an error arising with respect to another client's account.[44]

CONCLUSION

Governance, long an afterthought for most hedge funds and their managers, appears to be becoming more commonplace in the hedge fund business. Lurking behind the trend is a change in the type of investors holding interests in hedge funds and an increase in the level of regulation worldwide applied to the operations of hedge funds and their managers.

1 Lee Conrad, "Funds: Lousy Corporate Governance? No Problem. New fund will short the stock and wait for the fall," *US Banker*, July 1, 2004; Jaqueline Simmons and Katherine Burton, *Hedge Fund Managers Shake Up European Companies, Stoke Returns*, www.bloomberg.com, August 19, 2005.

2 *See* Jenny Anderson, "Lessons From Two Wrecked Hedge Funds," *New York Times*, September 9, 2005, at C1. *See also* Letter from Managed Funds Association on Prohibited Transaction Reform under ERISA, to The Honorable John A. Boehner, Chairman, Committee on Education and the Workplace (on file with Managed Fund Association) June 3, 2005.

3 *See, eg*, Release 2333; Steve Zwick, "2006: Hedge Funds Get Regulated," *Managed Money Futures*, December 1, 2005 (commenting that "[t]he United Kingdom's Financial Services Authority and Hong Kong's Monetary Authority are just two of several regional regulators set to unveil new rules for hedge funds in 2006....").

4 Alan Murray, "Hedge Funds are New Sheriffs of Boardroom," *Wall Street Journal*, December 14, 2005, at A2.

5 *See* Robert C. Pozen (2005) *The Mutual Fund Business* (Cambridge, MA: MIT Press) p. 559 for a discussion of the Wall Street rule.

6 *See* Gregory Zuckerman, "Big Shareholders are Shouting Even Louder – Activists Pressure Executives to Unlock Value, Even Using Pirate, Bulldog in their Monikers," *Wall Street Journal*, November 23, 2005, at C1; Stephen Taub, "Hedge Funds Flex Muscles, Exact Governance Changes," *Compliance Week*, May 10, 2005.

7 The SEC has said that a hedge fund manager would typically be an "investment adviser" as defined in the Advisers Act. The US Supreme Court in an oft-cited case, *SEC v Capital Gains Research Bureau, Inc.*, 375 US 180 (1963), articulated the view that an Advisers Act-registered

investment adviser is a fiduciary. Laws of other jurisdictions are in accord; the directors of a hedge fund formed under Cayman Islands law, eg, are deemed fiduciaries subject to a duty to act honestly and in good faith in the interest of the fund as English law informs the analysis. *Re Barings plc (5)* 1999 1 BCLC 433; Sean Scott, "Side Letters and Offshore Hedge Funds," *HFA* (22 August 2005). *See* Tamar Frankel, "Fiduciary Law," 71 *Calif. L. Rev.* 795, 809 (May 1983).

8 See *Goldstein*.

9 See *In Re Arleen W. Hughes*, SEC Exchange Act Release No. 4048 (February 18, 1948).

10 See *infra* note 5, Pozen Chapter 7 "Institutional Investors: The Reluctant Activists" at 572.

11 The SEC accepted this type of cost-benefit analysis when it adopted a rule under the Advisers Act relating to a registered investment adviser's voting proxies on behalf of its clients. "Proxy Voting by Investment Advisers," SEC Advisers Act Release No. 2106 (January 31, 2003). In particular, the SEC noted that a registered adviser may determine that not taking action may be in its client's best interest. In requiring advisers that exercise voting authority with respect to their client securities to adopt written proxy voting policies and procedures as part of that adviser's fiduciary duty, the SEC stated its acknowledgement that "[t]here may even be times when refraining from voting a proxy is in the client's best interest, such as when the adviser determines that the cost of voting the proxy exceeds the expected benefit to the client" *Id*.

12 Under these rules, a hedge fund seeking to present a proposal for a proxy contest with respect to a portfolio company at a meeting of the company's shareholders must have continuously held at least US$2,000 in market value, or 1%, of the company's securities entitled to be voted on the proposal at the meeting, for at least one year by the date on which the proposal is submitted. In addition, the hedge fund must continue to hold those securities through the date of the meeting at which the vote occurs. *See* Exchange Act Rule 14a-8.

13 In the US, such information is referred to as "material, nonpublic" information. See Section 204A of the Advisers Act.

14 *See, eg, SEC v. Hilary L. Shane*, SEC Litigation Release No 19227, Civil Action No 05 CIVIL 4772 (SDNY) (May 18, 2005); *SEC v. Langley Partners, LP, North Olmsted Partners, LP, Quantico Partners, LP, and Jeffrey Thorp*, SEC Litigation Release No.19607, Civil Action No 1:06CV00467 (JDB) (DDC) (14 March 2006); *SEC v. Michael K.C. Tom*, et al, SEC Litigation Release No 19404, (DC Mass), CA No 05-CV-11966-NMG (September 29, 2005).

15 Section 16 of the Exchange Act.

16 *See* Section 14(d) of the Exchange Act.

17 See Section 14(c) of the Exchange Act.

18 Typical state takeover statutes include the "freeze" or "business combination" statute, the "control acquisition" statute, and the "fair price" statute. A freeze statute delays any transaction that would complete the second step of a two-step acquisition in which the first step was not agreed to by target company's management. *See, eg, NY Bus. Corp. Law* § 912 (McKinney 2006). A control acquisition statute requires that acquiring persons holding controlling interests in the target company to deliver to the target company a disclosure statement describing the proposed acquisition. The target company's board then has a specified number of days to call a special shareholders' meeting. At that meeting, the transaction requires approval of a majority of the disinterested shares not owned or controlled by the acquiring person or any affiliate. *See, eg, Ohio Rev. Code Ann.* § 1701.831 (Baldwin Supp. 2006). A fair price takeover statute generally requires any takeover be approved by a specified percentage of the shares of a company's stock unless all shareholders receive the best price paid by the acquiring person within a designated period. *See, eg, Md. Code Ann., Corps. & Assns.* §§ 3-602, 3-603 (2006).

19 Gregory Zuckerman and Susan Pulliam, "Big Hedge Funds Are Seeking New Buyers – In Significant Shift in Strategy, They Reopen Doors to Investors in Bid to Generate Higher Fees," *Wall Street Journal*, September 24, 2005, at B1.

20 *See* Stephen Davis and John Lukomnik, "'Who Are These Guys?' Welcome to the Hedge Fund Era", *Compliance Week* (April 5, 2005).

21 *See* "Hedge Funds at the Gate", *Citigroup Global Corporate Finance Financial Strategy*, (September 22, 2005).

22 The action in Germany caused the head of German's ruling Social Democratic Party to call hedge funds "swarms of locusts that descend on companies". Julia Kollewe and Damian Reece, *Germany: Hedge Funds Accused of Ripping Heart Out of Economy*, www.corpwatch.org (May 11, 2005).

23 *See* Stephen Taub, "Proxy Battle Shows Firms' Clout; Not Afraid of a Fight," *Compliance Week*, June 15, 2004. In discussing hedge fund mogul Carl Icahn's tactics in investing in a company, a union representative observed, "[h]e looks to make a lot of money in a short period of time…[h]ow sincere is he for the long term?"

24 *Id*.

25 Peter V. Rajsingh, "Other Views: Well-Governed Hedge Funds Will Be a Cut Above the Rest; 'It's a mistake to equate transparency about governance with needing to reveal intricate details of proprietary trading strategies'," *Investment News*, May 3, 2004.

26 *See* Riva D. Atlas & Mary William Walsh, "Pension Officers Putting Billions into Hedge Funds," *Global Action on Aging*, November 27, 2005, *at* www.globalaging.org/pension/us/private/2005/hedgefunds.htm

27 "Testimony Concerning Investor Protection and the Regulation of Hedge Fund Advisers Before the US Senate Committee on Banking, Housing, and Urban Affairs," 108th Congr. (2004) testimony of William H. Donaldson, Chairman, US Securities and Exchange Commission).

28 See Hedge Fund Report at 68.

29 Directors may, be asked to approve principal securities transactions between the fund's manager and its fund.

30 *See supra* note 3. Under this rule, the method by which private fund advisers counted "clients" was effectively changed to require these advisers to count the investors in the private fund as the adviser's clients, rather than the hedge fund itself. If a hedge fund adviser manages funds that have, in total, more than 14 investors, the adviser becomes subject to the Advisers Act's registration requirements, unless the funds meet specified criteria, such as requiring a "two-year lock-up" of the investors' interests in the fund. This Rule was vacated in *Goldstein*.

31 Advisers Act Section 203(b).

32 In overseeing the application of the Advisers Act and its rules, the staff of the SEC will periodically examine and inspect the operation of hedge fund managers and their funds. The staff of the SEC conducted similar examinations prior to adopting the hedge fund manager registration rule. Of those examinations, the staff of the SEC has said that it "…believe[s] that the prospect of a compliance examination by the Commission staff will result in the adoption of procedures and controls designed to fulfill the hedge fund adviser's fiduciary responsibilities to the hedge fund and its investors." *See* note 28 at 110 (citing Neil Wilson, "Why Regulation Can Be Good," *Absolute Return* (April 2003) (noting that the UK regulation of fund advisers establishes minimum standards of practice, and that the process of registration encourages advisers to build professional operations before launching a fund "rather than scrambling to put them together after launch.")

33 Advisers Act Rule 206(4)-7.

34 The SEC has said that the chief compliance officer should be competent and knowledgeable and should be empowered with sufficient authority to enforce the manager's compliance policies. "Compliance Programs of Investment Companies and Investment Advisers," SEC Advisers Act Release No. 2204 (December 17, 2003).

35 *See* "2005 Sound Practices for Hedge Fund Managers" ("Sound Practices"), *Managed Funds Association* (2005).

36 An "access person" for these purposes is a supervised person of the manager who has access to nonpublic information regarding clients' purchases or sales of securities, who is involved in making securities recommendations to clients or who has access to securities recommendations that are non-public. All of a manager's directors, partners and officers are presumed to be "access persons". *See* Advisers Act Rule 204A-1(e)(1).

37 "Custody of Funds or Securities of Clients by Investment Advisers," Advisers Act Release 2176 (September 25, 2003).

38 Advisers Act Rule 206(4)-3.

39 *See* Advisers Act Rule 206(4)-1.

40 *See* Advisers Act Section 202(a)(1), which defines the term to include the direct or indirect transfer of a contracting block of the adviser's outstanding voting securities.

41 *See* Advisers Act Section 206(3) (stating that this prohibition against principal transactions undertaken without consent applies to any investment adviser, whether or not registered).

42 *Infra* note 10.

43 *Id.*

44 *See In re M & I Investment Mgmt. Corp.*, Advisers Act Release 1318 (June 30, 1992).

8

Key Tax and Accounting Issues

Diya Agarwal, Debbie Anthony,
Patrick Connolly, Robert Mirsky

Deloitte & Touche LLP

The previous chapters have reviewed several aspects of the relationship between hedge funds and prime brokers. In this chapter, we intend to discuss some of the various accounting and tax issues that need to be considered by all hedge fund businesses.

TAX ISSUES
UK corporate tax issues impacting hedge funds

In this section, we will consider the various issues that both the offshore funds (non-US hedge funds) and UK managers need to consider when managing a hedge fund business. We will outline the main UK corporate tax issues that should continually be reviewed by the directors of both operations.

Offshore funds

Where a UK investment manager is involved, a particular concern is whether the funds profits or gains could be subject to UK tax either because the fund itself could be managed in such a way that it is treated as resident in the UK for UK tax or because the activity of the investment manager in the UK constitutes a taxable presence (permanent establishment (PE)) of the fund in the UK.

Residence

Under UK domestic legislation, a company which is resident in the UK is chargeable to UK corporation tax on its worldwide income. A company may be UK resident if it is either incorporated in the

UK or if its "central management and control" is exercised in the UK. Therefore, in the case of a company incorporated overseas (eg, Cayman Islands or Bermuda), in determining whether or not the company is subject to UK corporation tax on its profits, it is crucial to identify by whom and where the central management and control of the company is exercised.

Given the above, it is possible for a company to be resident in more than one jurisdiction. Where this is the case and a tax treaty exists between an offshore jurisdiction and the UK, some protection regarding residence may be achieved. However the UK does not have relevant tax treaty agreements with the jurisdictions (principally tax neutral jurisdictions) such as the Cayman Islands and Bermuda which are popular locations of funds.

The "central management and control" concept is not defined by legislation although there are a number of principles that have been established as a result of cases going through the courts. Typically a company constitution (ie, the articles of association) will provide that the directors are responsible for managing the company and as such the central management and control ("CM&C") often resides where the board of directors exercise those powers ie, where they meet, although this is not conclusive.

The UK tax authorities, in their published guidance attempt to summarise the courts interpretation and states that the location of Board meetings, although important, is not the only determinant of the CM&C of a company. In some cases CM&C is exercised by a single person (ie, when a chairman or managing director exercises such powers and the board members are little more than ciphers). In other cases CM&C may be exercised by the shareholders.

The guidance provided by HM Customs & Excise ("HMR&C") also states that where there are doubts in regards to the residence of a company, the Inspector should:

❑ seek to ascertain whether the directors of the company in fact exercise CM&C;
❑ if they do so, seek to determine where the directors exercise this CM&C (which is not necessarily where they meet); and
❑ where directors apparently do not exercise CM&C of the company, look to establish where and by whom it is exercised.

As such, residence is a question of fact and in relation to the hedge fund industry is a well publicised area which is increasingly targeted by HMR&C. A number of recent cases have highlighted the following points:

❑ the burden of proving residence (or more specifically non-UK residence) lies with the taxpayer;
❑ the importance of good record and documentation retention; and
❑ the importance of local directors (and trustees) being kept informed of arrangements understanding the issues and making effective decisions.

The recent case *Wood and another v Holden (HM Inspector of Taxes)* is of particular interest. The case involves the issue of residence of two main offshore companies which were an essential part of a complex structure used to avoid capital gains tax. The case turned on central management and control.

HMR&C were not granted leave to appeal the case to the House of Lords and as such the Court of Appeal's decision in favour of the taxpayer was final. The case highlighted the importance of establishing whether or not CM&C is exercised through a company's "constitutional organs" (the board of directors or the general meeting) or whether those functions had effectively been usurped in the sense that CM&C are exercised independently of, or without regard to, those constitutional organs.

To help ensure that a fund does not become UK tax resident, the fund should:

❑ have a majority of appropriately qualified non-UK resident directors;
❑ ensure that all board meetings are attended in person (as opposed to by conference call) by the directors in a location outside the UK and preferably in the location of the incorporation of the fund; and
❑ discuss matters of genuine substance at the board meetings and take decisions thereon. It is important that the decisions are taken offshore and not merely rubber stamped at the board meetings.

A HMR&C inquiry into tax residence is both onerous and thorough. Not only are board papers reviewed, a detailed investigation may include reviews of e-mail correspondence, telephone records, airline tickets, etc. In general, when the hedge fund group is initially set up, appropriate procedures are put in place to ensure that any fund residence query could be robustly defended. Over time procedures may become less rigorously applied. Consistent monitoring of the residence position is therefore recommended.

The concept of CM&C for UK tax residence purposes applies equally to funds set up as partnership/look through entities rather than as corporate entities.

UK tax position of a non-UK resident fund

Even when a fund is non-UK resident, if it is carrying on a trade in the UK through a branch or agency, the profits or gains which arise will, prima facie, be subject to UK tax. The first point to consider therefore is whether the fund is trading or not.

Trading versus investment

If a non-resident is not "trading" (normally feeder funds would not be regarded as trading as they generally only hold a long term interest in the master fund) then it is only subject to UK income tax on UK source income and then only to the extent that the tax is deducted at source.

However, many other funds, including master funds, adopt strategies which would generally be regarded as trading. A UK based investment manager which has discretionary authority to conclude trades on the funds behalf would in these circumstances be regarded as carrying on the trade of the non-resident fund in the UK. As such, the analysis as to whether the non-resident is trading or not is essential.

In UK tax legislation, there is no definition of "trading". Instead, the meaning is an issue that must be decided on its own facts. The courts over the years have relied on examining the facts and looking for a presence or absence of common features or characteristics of trade. As case law has developed in the UK such characteristics have developed to create the "badges of trade". The number of transactions; the nature of the assets; the nature of any enhancements made to the asset; the circumstances of sale; and, the passage of time between the purchase and sale are all factors which would be taken into account.

For an offshore hedge fund carrying out a large volume of transactions over a short period of time, such characteristics would typically resemble a trading activity. It is known that the UK tax authorities also consider the ability of a fund to hold short positions to be indicative of a trading activity.

However, even if a fund is treated as carrying on a trade rather than investment activity, the UK manager can avoid being assessed UK tax on the profits it generates for the offshore fund provided the conditions of the investment manager exemption ("IME") are satisfied.

Investment Manager Exemption conditions
In order to be able to fall under this exemption (and as such avoid the profits and gains of the offshore company being subject to UK corporation tax) it is essential that all the transactions being carried out by the UK investment manager on behalf of the fund must arise from an "investment transaction" as defined in the UK tax legislation. The term, as might be expected, includes transactions in securities and most derivative transactions – but not where the underlying property is land. Commodities where there could be physical settlement are also not included whilst whether carbon emission credit trades fall within the definitions is not clear. Perhaps however the area where there is greatest uncertainty is loan originations. Some argue that this falls within the definition as it is "placing money on deposit" whilst it is known that the UK tax authorities take the view that such transactions fall outside the scope of the definition. Given the complexity and sophistication of investment strategies being adopted by hedge funds, it is not always clear whether or not certain transactions will fall under this definition and whether the wording in the legislation is suitably flexible. The UK tax authorities however are concerned that if the definition is too flexible it may have unintended consequences with other financial players taking advantage of provisions that are aimed at providing an environment which facilitates the growth and smooth operation of the UK investment management industry. Representations have been made to the UK Revenue authorities concerning the application of the investment management exemption in general which includes recommendations to widen the scope of transactions covered by the exemption.

HMR&C have indicated that the IME is under review and anticipate issuing a new Statement of Practice in Autumn 2006.

Provided the transactions undertaken by the UK manager fall within the definition of investment transactions, there are six main conditions that need to be satisfied by the UK manager for full availability of the IME. They are:

❑ at the time of the transaction the UK manager is carrying on a business of providing investment management services;

❑ the relevant transactions are carried out by the UK manager in the ordinary course of its business;

❑ the UK manager acts on behalf of the non-resident in an "independent capacity" – the "independence test" (see below);

❑ over a period of not more than five years, including the year in question, the UK manager (and any other connected person) should not have a beneficial entitlement of 20% or more of the aggregate profit of the offshore fund derived from the UK manager's activities – the "20% rule" (see below);

❑ the remuneration received by the UK manager is "not less than that which would be customary for the class of business concerned"; and

❑ the UK manager is not treated as a PE (taxable presence) of the non-resident in relation to any other transaction in the same period.

The two conditions that tend to cause most concern are the "independence test" and the "20% test" and the structuring of funds and management companies need to be carefully considered in order to ensure these two conditions will be satisfied.

The independence test may be satisfied in a number of ways. Generally where the fund is established as a company then the test will be satisfied if it is a "widely held collective fund" (ie, the majority of the fund is not held by five or fewer persons or not more than 20% of the fund is held by one person). Alternatively, the fund may be listed on a recognised exchange. The test will also be considered to be satisfied if the investment managers services are provided to more than one unconnected funds such that not more than 70% of the UK manager's fees are received from any one fund.

The 20% test seeks to prevent individuals using the exemption to structure a private "hedge fund" vehicle solely for the manager and with the purpose of avoiding UK taxation. The management and performance fees received by the UK manager and its connected parties are not included in any calculations of the 20% threshold provided those fees would have been allowed as a deduction when the fund's taxable profits are calculated (which would seem to put funds established as look through entities at a disadvantage). It should be noted however that if the 20% threshold is breached but the independence test is satisfied, then any profits of the funds to which third parties are entitled would not be assessed on the UK manager. Moreover the test is treated as satisfied where the investment manager took reasonable steps to achieve the condition and the failure to do so was beyond its control.

The IME is an essential part of the UK tax legislation for hedge funds and has allowed the hedge fund industry to grow significantly in the UK. As such it is very important to obtain a good understanding of how the conditions could apply to a structure in order to ensure any hedge fund business is commercially viable.

Taxation of investors
To the extent that an offshore hedge fund has UK resident investors then unless the fund has distributor tax status in the UK (which is generally not the case), any profits which arise on the disposal by the investors of their interest in the fund will be subject to UK income tax rules rather than capital gains tax rules. This is particularly relevant for individual investors as they will generally pay a higher effective rate of tax on such gains. To obtain distributor status, broadly, the fund must distribute at least 85% of the fund's taxable income calculated on a UK equivalent basis in each accounting period. For most funds this would be impractical.

If a UK company invests in an offshore fund where broadly 60% of the market value of the fund comprises debt instruments then it is likely that the company's interest in the fund will be taxed on a mark to market basis regardless of whether the fund has distributor status or not.

UK manager

Structure

The establishment of fund management operations in the UK would create a UK taxable presence and is also likely to require regulatory permission.

There are several ways that a UK manager can set up operations in the UK. The three main possibilities are either as a branch, a limited company or a partnership.

Setting up as a branch of an overseas entity usually avoids the need for the entity to have a statutory UK audit (*see* audit section). However for regulatory purposes, the entity as a whole would be subject to UK regulation which could lead to additional costs. It is uncommon in the industry for hedge fund businesses to set up operations in the UK as a branch. It is more customary for fund managers to either set up as a limited company or a partnership.

Partnership structures have become an increasingly popular choice of investment management vehicle since 2001 when the concept of a limited liability partnership ("LLP") was introduced into UK law. This is a corporate entity which for UK tax purposes is regarded as a transparent or look-through entity. This means that the members of the LLP (ie, the partners) are not regarded as employees but instead are subject to income tax on their share of the LLP's profits. This can be an attractive structure if it is intended that all profits are paid out rather than retained in the business as it not only reflects the relationships the key personnel have with one another but also the national insurance payable on partners' drawings can be significantly less than the amount payable on the same amount paid as salaries and bonuses for an employee. On the other hand, a corporate entity is often simpler to administer and may be more tax efficient if profits are retained in the business. Ultimately, the most appropriate structure will depend upon the facts and circumstances of each individual case.

Transfer pricing – research/advisory/discretionary management

The UK transfer pricing rules and documentation requirements apply to transactions with associated entities under common control (and in some cases also to 40% joint venture type arrangements), and the UK legislation is broadly worded to include partnerships as well as corporate entities into the regime. The UK rules follow OECD guidelines and as such documentation is required and must detail the nature of the transactions, the remuneration basis, why it is considered arm's length and independent third party comparables data. Penalties of up to 100% of tax underpaid can be incurred for failure to produce adequate documentation.

The key issue for hedge fund businesses is understanding where the key investment expertise is and whether that jurisdiction is receiving appropriate remuneration for work done. For UK purposes, the key issue is whether the UK is getting its fair share given the work that is being undertaken in the UK.

Where an overseas based group sets up in the UK for the first time they often set up a research activity, this may be followed by investment advisory service activities or full discretionary management activities.

Pure research functions where the research is provided to a non-UK investment manager are most often remunerated on a cost plus basis (the level of margin depending upon the extent of the operations of the company).

For investment advisory services, the appropriate remuneration basis again depends upon the nature and extent of the services provided. Where the UK operations are purely acting in an advisory capacity and the decision making is performed outside the UK by individuals with the appropriate level of expertise to make such decisions then a cost plus basis may be supportable. However, if the advisers had a very active role and it could be demonstrated that the majority of their recommendations were final, HMR&C may argue that a more appropriate method of remuneration might, for example be based on a split of the revenues received by the investment manager from the funds.

In the case of full discretionary management, where such activities are sub-delegated from the main investment manager of a fund, some form of revenue split is likely to be the most appropriate basis of remuneration.

A detailed review of the activities should always be undertaken in order to determine the most appropriate basis of remuneration for UK transfer pricing purposes. In the case of a UK company undertaking investment management services, this would be required both for transfer pricing purposes but also to determine that the level of remuneration is "not less than that which would be customary for the class of business concerned" (one of the conditions of the IME).

It should be noted that fund advisory and management businesses are being actively targeted for review by one of the UK Revenue's specialist tax offices (Special Civil Investigations office ("SCI")). Transfer pricing is one of the most common areas of settlement where the key concern is profits retained by offshore managers. It is therefore important to bear in mind that the transfer pricing position should be reviewed regularly and appropriate documentation supporting the pricing adopted should be retained.

Offshore arrangements project
HMR&C's "offshore arrangements" initiative was launched in 2003 in response to the perception that substantial tax leakage was occurring through various offshore structures.

The project insofar as it relates to the hedge fund sector involves major probes into:

❏ investment managers and investment advisors; and
❏ hedge funds.

As such, HMR&C's main concern is the adequacy of profits recognised in the UK in relation to the level of expertise and perceived activity in the UK. A particular concern arises when HMR&C believes that a majority of the profits generated remain in the offshore jurisdiction where it is not matched by the level of activity in the offshore jurisdiction.

The three main areas of attack are not unexpected:

❏ the residence status of the funds and fund manager;
❏ whether the fund is carrying on a trade in the UK through a branch, agency or permanent establishment; and
❏ transfer pricing.

Experience has shown that SCI will often examine the individuals (founders/principals) as part of, or even, a lead into an investigation of the structure as a whole. HMR&C believe that a close examination of the role and functions of the principals is an essential precursor to the investigation of the operation of the fund structure as it helps to identify who is doing what and where they are doing it.

If a hedge fund business does find that it is being investigated by the SCI, it is typical for the UK fund manager to first receive a letter indicating that an inquiry is about to commence. The letter will also detail a lengthy request for documents and information. At some stage during the investigation, there will almost certainly also be a request for an interview with the relevant directors.

While such investigations will be costly and time consuming for fund managers, they are not to be feared providing robust structures, appropriate documentation and well planned operations are maintained.

Offshore manager and PE risks

At the beginning of this chapter, the PE risks of the offshore fund were discussed in the context of a UK based investment manager. In many cases however portfolio managers based offshore make occasional visits to the UK. A frequent question is the length/regularity of the visits and the scope of the activity which may be undertaken before potentially creating either a PE of the offshore manager or fund in the UK. It should be noted that this is an extremely complex area and will be highly dependent upon the facts and circumstances of each individual case, consequently professional advice should always be sought.

The UK domestic legislation follows the OECD definition of a PE and states that a PE may be created if an only if:

❑ it has a fixed place of business through which the business of the company is wholly or partly carried on; or
❑ an agent acting on behalf of the company has and habitually exercises their authority to do business on behalf of the company.

In order not to create a PE by virtue of having a fixed place of business, it is important that the offshore manager does not have any office space in the UK allocated to it.

Assuming this is the case, then the agent (ie, an employee) of the offshore manager should not habitually exercise their authority in the UK on behalf of the offshore manager. Examples of this would include concluding contracts on behalf of the offshore manager in the UK.

To the extent that the activities of the employee of the offshore manager are only of a preparatory or auxiliary character, then no PE of the offshore manager will be deemed to exist in the UK. In the context of fund managers such activities would typically include informal visits to potential investors, marketing, advertising of services etc.

Where an employee of an offshore manager is spending time and exercising their authority in the UK for example, a portfolio manager taking decisions on trading positions/executing transactions etc, it is vital to consider whether such activity is "habitual". There is no definition in the UK tax legislation for "habitual" and as such whether authority is exercised habitually is a matter of consideration of all the facts and circumstances. For instance a portfolio manager based offshore who spends two weeks a year on holiday in the UK but reviews trading positions daily and takes decisions thereon is unlikely to be considered habitual, however spending two months a year in the UK on the same basis may well be considered habitual. Other factors such as the volume of the transactions undertaken would also need to be taken into account.

In conclusion, when setting up a fund with a UK investment manager there are a number of complex issues to address and monitor. Both the tax status of the fund manager and the fund itself needs to be considered and constantly monitored. The increased scrutiny of fund operations by HMR&C and the regulators in the UK highlight the importance of ensuring that any planning undertaken is robust in order to be able to stand up to any potential challenge from HMR&C.

THE US TAX SYSTEM

The US is an attractive place in which to invest, manage assets, and solicit investors. However, the US tax system is composed of a complicated set of rules that can adversely impact hedge funds, whether domiciled in the US or outside of the US.

This section of the chapter will give an overview of some of the US tax issues that hedge funds may encounter.

STRUCTURE
Master–feeder

A master–feeder structure is a common hedge fund structure used to decrease costs and increase investor access. Other fund structures that maintain separate asset pools may have some advantages such as lower set-up costs, but the efficiencies created in the master–feeder structure are often more attractive. A master–feeder structure allows US taxable investors to invest in a fund without compromising the tax position of other non-US investors or US tax-exempt investors.

As the name suggests, the structure of the fund consists of one master fund with numerous feeder funds that contribute assets into the master. In a US domiciled fund the feeder funds normally consist of one fund for US investors, one fund for foreign investors, and one entity setup by the manager to control or manage the entire fund. The master fund pools all the assets from the feeder funds and uses these assets to make the fund's investments. Pooling the assets of each fund in the master fund allows the manager to make collective investment decisions and avoid the time and expense of allocating trades between funds. Additional cost savings are created as third parties, such as accountants, attorneys, and bankers are able deal with one, rather than multiple funds. Having one larger pool of assets rather than two or more small pools creates better investment opportunities through greater leverage otherwise unavailable to smaller funds, such as derivatives trading, for example. However, establishing the fund may be more costly than other fund structures because of the need for additional audits and tax return filings.

The master fund is normally a corporate entity established in a tax neutral jurisdiction, like the Cayman Islands, that files an election under the US entity classification regulations (a Form 8832 also known as a "Check-the-Box" election), to be treated as a partnership for US federal income tax purposes. The master fund engages in the trading of the investments. The feeder entities are usually established as a US partnership for US investors and a foreign corporation for foreign and US tax-exempt investors. Foreign investors invest in the foreign corporation in order to avoid any detrimental US tax and regulatory impact, while US tax exempt investors invest through foreign corporations to avoid potential exposure to US tax imposed on "unrelated business taxable income" or "UBTI", as discussed below.

Alternative master–feeder

The alternative master–feeder structure is similar to the master–feeder without a US partnership through which US investors invest.

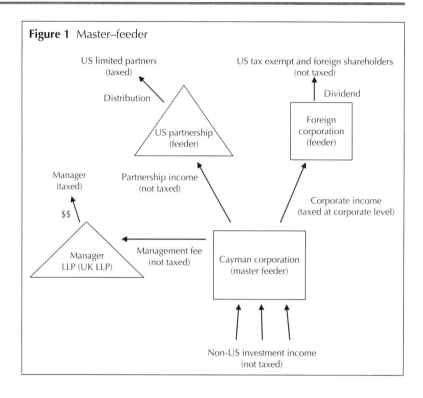

Figure 1 Master–feeder

While tax implications on this structure are similar to those in the master–feeder structure some investors fear the impact of potential US regulation of the fund and commingling of assets with US taxable investors.

ENTITIES
Partnerships
Partnerships are generally treated as conduit entities and, therefore, not subject to US federal income taxation. The various items of partnership income, gains and losses, etc, flow through to the individual partners and are reported on the partners' personal income tax returns. Partnerships have the ability to allocate ordinary income, capital gains, losses, and deductions among the partners as they see fit (subject to certain restrictions imposed under US law). US partnerships may be utilised in the master–feeder structure.

US partnership compliance requires the annual filing of a Form 1065, US Return of Partnership Income ("Form 1065"). In turn, the

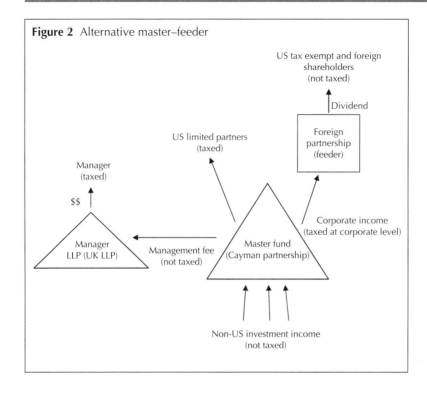

Figure 2 Alternative master–feeder

Form 1065 requires the filing of individual partner forms, known as a Schedule K-1, for the US partners. Generally, foreign partnerships that have gross income which is effectively connected with the conduct of a trade or business ("ECI") within the US or have gross income derived from sources in the US must also file a Form 1065, even if the partnership's principal place of business is outside the US (see discussion below).

Additionally, individual US partners must file a Form 8865, "Return of US Persons with Respect to Certain Foreign Partnerships" ("Form 8865") if at any time during the taxable year the US person owned a 10% or greater interest in a foreign partnership, and the foreign partnership is controlled by US persons who each hold a 10% or greater interest in the foreign partnership (referred to as a Controlled Foreign Partnership or "CFP"). The Form 8865 is also required to be filed if a US person's proportional interest in the foreign partnership changes by 10% or more or the US person's interest in the foreign partnership becomes greater or less than 10%.

In addition to being time consuming and costly to file, the Form 8865 requires disclosure of certain investments by the CFP, and certain transactions between the filer, the CFP, and other related entities. Some partners may be averse to disclosing this information to the US tax authorities.

Foreign corporations

As discussed, hedge funds often incorporate in no-tax, or low-tax, jurisdictions. A corporation, domestic or foreign, is generally treated as a separate legal entity for US federal income tax purposes. While the corporate form generally protects shareholders from current US federal income tax on income generated by the corporation, the income is usually subject to two levels of US taxation by the time the income is distributed to the shareholder.

Income of a foreign corporation earned outside of the US is generally not subject to US federal income tax; however, there are some situations where the foreign corporation, or its shareholders, are subject to current US taxation. US taxation may occur when a foreign corporation is engaged in a US trade or business, or if the foreign corporation has income which is effectively connected with the conduct of a trade or business within the US. A US federal income tax liability can also arise if the shareholder of a foreign corporation is a taxable US person, or, in some instances, a tax exempt US person which earns unrelated business taxable income. These concepts are discussed in detail below.

Additional tax reporting requirements may arise if more than 50% of the shares of a foreign corporation (tested by vote or value) is owned by US shareholders, each with a 10% or greater voting interest in the foreign corporation. These foreign corporations are referred to in the Internal Revenue Code as controlled foreign corporations ("CFCs"). Generally, US shareholders must include their pro-rata share of certain types of income earned by a CFC, referred to as "subpart F income" and earnings of the CFC that are invested in US property.

Even if a foreign corporation is not controlled by US persons but is engaged in a trade or business within the US and has income which is effectively connected with that US trade or business, the foreign corporation is required to file a Form 1120-F, US Income Tax Return of a Foreign Corporation ("Form 1120-F").

US shareholders or officers of a foreign corporation may also be required to file Form 5471, Information Return of US Persons with Respect to Certain Foreign Corporations ("Form 5471"), if the US person is an officer, director or 10% shareholder of a foreign corporation. Certain additional share acquisitions or disposals of shares of a controlled foreign corporation may also result in the requirement to file Form 5471.

OFFSHORE ENTITY CONSIDERATIONS
US trade or business

Offshore hedge funds should also be aware of what US tax implications may exist with respect to the formation, operation or liquidation of a fund. As mentioned above, foreign corporations are generally subject to US federal income tax on income that is effectively connected with the conduct of a trade or business within the US, with certain exceptions.[1] The concept of "effectively connected income" can create problems as many hedge funds invest in US business in varying capacities.

Generally, a foreign corporation will be subject to US federal income tax on income derived from a US trade or business. While case law has developed the concept, the IRS rarely issues guidance on the analysis of whether income is derived from a US trade or business. However, it is a factual determination and courts have ruled that a foreign corporation's US economic activities that are "considerable, continuous, and regular" are indicative of trade or business.[2]

Foreign investors are protected from being subject to US federal income tax (but not US withholding tax) on interest, dividends or most other fund returns as courts have distinguished the activities of "investing" from those of "trading," where trading is defined as buying and selling securities with a reasonable frequency in an effort to make a short-term profit on the daily market movements.[3] Further, tax exempt investors have statutory protection from being subject to US federal income tax on their investment activities.

Until the 1960s, the application of trade or business to the trading of stocks and securities was not uniform across the judicial landscape of the US, and Congress moved to clarify the concept. The underlying goal was to avoid impeding foreign investment into the US as a result of aggressive taxation.

Safe harbours

Congress' solution was to create two safe harbours for trading stocks, securities, and commodities. These safe harbours include protection for options, futures, and other derivatives.[4]

Generally, an offshore hedge fund may trade in stocks, securities, or commodities through a resident broker, commission agent, custodian or other independent agent, other than through an office or fixed place of business in the US.[5] Known as the "dealer" safe harbour, the statutory protection fails if the hedge fund has an office or fixed place of business in the US at any time during the taxable year. The dealer safer harbour protects a dealer trading stocks, securities, and commodities from being engaged in a "US trade or business".

Additionally, an offshore hedge fund can trade in stocks, securities or commodities by itself, through an employee, or through a broker, commission agent, custodian, or other agent, whether dependent or independent, resident or non-resident, present or not present in the US.[6] Known as the "trading" safe harbour, the critical difference between it and the dealer safe harbour is that the trading safe harbour applies to trades made for the hedge fund's own account.

One important exception to the safe harbours is the taxability of real property transactions.[7] Gain or loss arising from transactions in real property located within the US or the US Virgin Islands will be considered to be effectively connected with the conduct of a trade or business within the US. No distinction is made for property held for business, investment, or personal use and therefore gains arising from the sale or exchange of any US real property interest may be subject to US federal income tax. The provision also applies to transactions in the shares of certain US corporations which principally hold US real property.

US entity classification provisions

Generally, an offshore fund can elect to treat certain foreign entities as transparent or as a corporation for US federal income tax purposes. Upon election, the foreign entity will be subject to the relevant US compliance requirements applicable to the type of entity which results from the election.

The election, commonly referred to as a "check-the-box" election is made on Form 8832, Entity Classification Election ("Form

8832") and must include the employer identification number ("EIN") of the entity which is the subject of the election. If the entity does not have an EIN, it must file a Form SS4, "Application for Employer Identification Number" ("Form SS4"), along with the Form 8832.

Generally, the election must be made within 75 days of the desired effective date and cannot be changed for 60 months following the effective date of the election. One important exception to this rule applies where an election is made at the time of formation. This election, referred to as an "initial classification election" can be changed at any time thereafter without limitation. Most foreign entities can make the election; however, there are certain *per se* entities that will only be treated as corporations for US federal income tax purposes and whose status as a corporation cannot be changed.

Passive foreign investment company ("PFIC")

Offshore funds will also need to be aware of the US passive foreign investment company ("PFIC") rules that can result in adverse US federal income tax consequences to certain US shareholders. In brief, US shareholders of a PFIC are generally subject to US federal income tax arising from the disposal of shares of a PFIC or the receipt of a significant distribution from a PFIC as well as an interest charge. The interest charge is imposed on the US tax imposed, computed as if the tax had accrued rateably over the holding period of the shares. Alternatively, the PFIC shareholders may elect to pay current US federal income tax on their respective share of the income of the PFIC. The PFIC tax regime is particularly onerous and complex.

Two scenarios will cause a foreign corporation to become a PFIC. A foreign corporation will be a PFIC if 75% or more of its gross income in the corporation's taxable year is passive income. Or, a foreign corporation will be a PFIC if 50% or more of the average value of the assets held by the foreign corporation in a particular taxable year are held for the production of passive income.

Passive income will generally be dividends, interest, royalties, rents, annuities, net gains on sales of property producing passive income, and other income classified as foreign personal holding company income for purposes of Internal Revenue Code of 1986 as Amended ("code").[8]

PFIC status is dangerous because once a foreign corporation qualifies as a PFIC with respect to a shareholder, it will generally continue to be a PFIC with respect to that shareholder even if the foreign corporation no longer fits within the definition of a PFIC. However, there are ways to purge the PFIC taint. A US shareholder of a PFIC can manage the holding in one of three ways.

QEF

A shareholder that elects to treat the foreign corporation as a Qualified Electing Fund ("QEF") is taxed annually on a rateable share of the corporation's earnings, regardless of whether the earnings were actually distributed. Note again, it is the shareholder, not the fund that makes this election.

While the shareholder does not get the advantage of deferral under this method, this method may be advantageous because there will not be interest charged on the deferred earnings when the shareholder sells its stock or when the shareholder receives distributions from the corporation. Under the QEF election, the shareholder's pro-rata share of ordinary earnings is ordinary income, and the net capital gain is long-term capital gain. If the opportunity to make a QEF election exists, it is generally advisable due to the high interest charge on excess distributions.

A disadvantage to this regime is that the PFIC, and each intermediary through which a shareholder owns PFIC stock, must provide the shareholder with a PFIC annual information statement.[9] This statement contains information that the IRS has deemed necessary to administer the PFIC rules. These annual statements can be burdensome, and not supplying the information statement may result in the IRS invalidating or terminating the QEF election.

Excess distribution

A shareholder that makes no election is subject to special rules when an excess distribution from the PFIC or a disposition of stock occurs. An excess distribution is generally a distribution in the current tax year that is greater than 125% of the average distributions received in respect to such stock by the shareholder during the preceding tax years. However, no part of a distribution received or deemed received during the first tax year of the shareholder's holding period of the stock will be treated as an excess distribution.

This method potentially results in substantial tax arising upon the disposition of the shares in a PFIC because the US federal income tax imposed at the highest marginal rate and is calculated as if the gain accrued ratably over the investment's holding period. The total tax due will be the sum of the yearly taxes due plus interest which is imposed on that amount from each year's tax due date.

Mark-to-market election

Shareholders of PFIC stock that is regularly traded on a qualified exchange or other market may elect to "mark-to-market" their holding. Under this election the electing shareholder must annually report the amount by which the fair market value of the PFIC stock at year-end exceeds the taxpayer's basis for the stock as income.[10] Under the election, the US taxpayer includes this amount as ordinary income. Further, any gain on disposal is recognised as ordinary income, and loss on disposition is deductible as an ordinary loss to the extent of net mark-to-market gains. The shareholder basis in its stock is adjusted to reflect any mark to market inclusions or deductions.

This method may be advantageous because it does not require an annual information statement to be provided by the PFIC, and it does not result in the punitive tax treatment of the deferred interest method.

Shareholders of a PFIC must file Form 8621, "Return by a Shareholder of a Passive Foreign Investment Company or Qualified Electing Fund" ("Form 8621"), for each tax year that the shareholder recognises gain on disposition of the PFIC stock, receives a distribution from the PFIC, or is making an election with respect to the PFIC stock.

Shareholders of a PFIC that have made a QEF election must also provide a PFIC annual information statement that enables the shareholder to correctly calculate the taxable earnings of the QEF for US federal income tax purposes. Failure to provide the IRS with the information statement will likely cause the QEF election to fail.

It is important to note that tax-exempt investors are generally not affected by PFIC rules because the rules do not make income taxable if the income was not previously taxable. Further, only US shareholders are subject to PFIC rules. The appropriate PFIC election must be made by the shareholder, and is not made by the foreign corporation. However, the shareholder is responsible for acquiring the PFIC annual information statement.

Subpart F income

As mentioned above, US persons must include their pro-rata share of a CFC's subpart F income in their personal income tax return. Subpart F triggers tax reporting requirements for US shareholders of a CFC if the foreign corporation was a CFC for 30 consecutive days during its tax year and that US shareholder owned stock in the foreign corporation on the last day of the year on which the foreign corporation was a CFC.[11] For purposes of this section of the Code, a US shareholder is a US person who owns 10% or more of the total combined voting power of all classes of voting stock in the corporation.[12]

There are several categories of Subpart F income, the most important of which is foreign base company income. Subpart F requires US shareholders to currently recognise income equal to their pro-rata share of a CFC's foreign base company income. The Code divides foreign base company income into several subcategories including foreign personal holding company income, foreign base company sales income, and foreign base company services income.[13] However, the latter two subcategories are not as applicable to most hedge funds.

Foreign personal holding company income is specific income earned from passive activities. IRC Section 954 defines personal holding company income to include income from dividends, interest, rents, royalties, and annuities. Foreign personal holding company income also includes net gains from commodities transactions, foreign currency transactions, and income from notional principal contracts.

UBTI

US tax-exempt investors in offshore funds may run the risk of being responsible for UBTI. UBTI is gross income generated by a US tax exempt organisation from an unrelated trade or business regularly carried on by the tax-exempt organisation, less the allowable deductions incurred while carrying on the trade or business. Generally, unrelated trade or business is any trade or business which is not substantially related to the exercise or performance by an organisation of its charitable, educational, or other purpose or function constituting the basis for its exemption.[14]

UBTI becomes important when US tax-exempt investors are engaged in leveraged activities where income arises from debt financed property. Debt financed property will be any debt-acquired property that is held to produce income.

Though the UBTI net was originally intended to capture real estate activities, its application to other activities is complex. Generally, the tax-exempt property will be subject to US tax on interest, dividends, rents, or sales generated by debt-financed property owned by the tax-exempt entity. The amount of income that must be included is the result of the average acquisition indebtedness divided by the average cost basis of the property, multiplied by the income from the property.

When tax-exempt investors invest in offshore limited partnerships, the pass-through status of partnerships will cause UBTI to pass through as well. An offshore "blocker" corporation may be used to shield tax-exempt investors from incurring UBTI. Under this plan, a blocker corporation is placed between the tax-exempt partner and the partnership, and the tax-exempt investors receive flow through dividend treatment from the blocker corporation not subject to UBTI.

A tax-exempt entity that incurs UBTI greater than US$1,000 in any taxable year must file a US federal tax return regardless of whether it has no tax liability for the year.

Withholding tax and tax credits

Generally, US source payments made to a foreign investor are subject to a 30% withholding tax. Payments that qualify as income subject to US withholding tax will be interest, dividends, rent, salaries, wages, premiums, annuities, compensations and remunerations. Withholding is required when the recipient is a foreign person, the amount paid is from a US source, the amount paid is fixed or determinable annual or periodical income ("FDAP") not effectively connected to US trade or business, the payor or an agent of the payor is a withholding agent, and no exceptions apply. Generally, the withholding agent will be the last person in the US who has custody of income before transferring it to a foreign person.

Portfolio interest exemption

Establishing themselves in low tax jurisdictions, hedge funds often attempt to minimise US tax consequences by physically staying out the US. However, as discussed above, funds that make investments in the United States may still be subject to US taxation. The portfolio interest exemption is a method commonly used by foreign taxpayers to exploit certain US investment opportunities without being subject to US withholding tax on interest payments. The policy purpose behind this exception is to encourage investment in US markets without corresponding negative tax consequences.

The portfolio interest exemption exempts FDAP characterised as "portfolio interest" from US withholding tax. Generally, portfolio interest is interest on debt that does not arise from an active business of the lender and is earned by an identifiable foreign person. Strict requirements are imposed in order to ensure that the interest is not a disguised return from an active trade or business and the recipients are not US persons. Interest on both registered bonds and bearer bonds can qualify for this exception; however, more requirements are imposed on bearer bond interest.

A registered bond does not need to be in written form to qualify for the portfolio interest exemption. "[A] book entry bond shall be treated as in registered form if the right to the principal of, and stated interest on, such bond may be transferred only through a book entry consistent with regulations prescribed by the secretary."[15] Following this guidance most entities have the ability to issue registered debt provided the debtor only pays interest and principal to an identifiable owner of record.

Due to the unmonitored transferability of bearer bonds, stricter requirements are imposed in order to fit them under this exemption. The interest on these bonds is exempt only if: (a) "there are arrangements reasonably designed to insure that such obligation will be sold (or resold) only to a person who is not a United States citizen"; (b) "interest on such obligation is payable only outside the United States and its possessions"; and (c) "on the face of such obligation there is a statement that any United States person who holds such obligation will be subject to limitations under the United States income tax laws".[16]

Exceptions to the withholding requirement

In addition to using the portfolio interest exemption, hedge funds can invest in certain other US interest producing vehicles and still be able to avoid withholding tax. Short-term Original Issue Discount (OID) and interest from "80/20" companies are notable exceptions.

The IRS imputes interest on particular types of bonds. When a debt instrument is issued at a lower price than the future redemption price, the IRS deems that difference to be interest and taxes it on an annual basis. For example, if an issuer issued a note for US$90 with a US$100 redemption price for a two year term the IRS would deem US$10 to be OID. That OID income, US$10, would be divided over the term of the note and taxed accordingly, US$5 income per year. Although no money is actually paid out until redemption, there is a withholding requirement if the OID is being paid to a non-US person.[17] However, there is an exception for short-term OID. Short-term OID is any debt obligation that is payable in 183 days or less from the date of original issue, though back to back short term obligations may not qualify.[18] This exception allows banks to issue commercial paper to foreign persons without imposing the withholding tax.

Additionally, dividends and interest paid by "80/20" companies may also be exempt from withholding. An "80/20" company is a domestic corporation that derives 80% or more of its gross income from the active conduct of a foreign business during the three year prior test period.[19] Interest paid from these companies is considered foreign source income and not subject to withholding tax. Dividends paid from these companies are also potentially exempt from withholding tax. Once the payor meets the 80% threshold, the exempt portion equals the amount of the dividend times the ratio of foreign source gross income for that period.[20]

MANAGER TAX CONCERNS

US managers of hedge funds outside the US will be taxed on their income earned regardless of where that income is earned, subject to tax treaties and foreign tax credits. Further, managers that are not US Citizens will be taxed on their income that is effectively connected with a US trade or business, subject to exceptions. FDAP income will be withheld at the source at a 30% rate.

Hedge funds managers face potentially two levels of US taxation, federal and state. However, persons that work in New York City may have a third level of taxation imposed upon them, the unincorporated business tax. This tax is levied on every individual, unincorporated entity or incorporated entity treated as a partnership for federal income tax purposes that engages in a trade or business in New York City and earns more that US$75,000. The tax is assessed on any unincorporated entity that carries out a trade or business in New York City, regardless of whether or not that entity is a resident of New York City. The 4% tax rate is assessed on any amount of income allocated to trade or business activities carried out in the City.

Hedge funds and hedge fund managers must be mindful of this tax as they can be subject to this tax by any actions that are deemed to rise to the level of a trade or business in the City. Though hedge fund managers have distanced themselves from this tax by managing offshore hedge funds from offices established outside of New York City, a permanent physical presence in the City is not determinative. As the world's largest financial capital New York promises access to a wealth of potential fund investors. Soliciting potential fund investors in New York City could likely be considered carrying on a trade or business and therefore be taxable to the fund manager at a 4% rate.

Fund domiciles

The default jurisdiction for hedge funds is the Cayman Islands. Approximately 80% of the world's hedge funds are registered with CIMA. The Cayman Islands has many features that attract hedge funds: political and social stability, business friendly environment, attractive tax regime, and industry expertise. However, even though the Cayman Islands is considered a tax neutral territory and imposes no direct income or capital gains tax, many of the funds domiciled in the Cayman Islands must still comply with external taxing agencies, such as the US IRS, depending on which taxing regime the funds' investors fall.

Some other offshore centres that funds domicile in are Jersey, Bermuda, British Virgin Islands, Guernsey and the Isle of Man. Additionally, Dublin and Luxembourg are popular locations to domicile for institutional investors who require EU registration.

EU ISSUES
EU Savings Tax Directive

The European Union ("EU") Savings Tax Directive (with its associated agreements, "Directive"), specifically, the Council Directive 2003/48/EC on Taxation of Savings Income in the Form of Interest Payments, came into force on 1st July, 2005, with the aim of preventing EU resident individuals from escaping tax on interest[21] received cross-border.

Under this regime, paying agents[22] in the EU member states and dependent and associated territories and certain named "third" countries (together, "relevant jurisdictions") are required to report to their domestic tax authority details of the payments they make. This information is then passed on to the tax authority where the individual is resident. However, in some jurisdictions, usually where banking secrecy laws prevail, paying agents are required to withhold tax from the payments they make instead of reporting information. The tax will usually be credited against the individual's domestic tax liability. Alternatively, the individual usually has the option of requesting exchange of information instead of withholding.

As part of its anti-avoidance aims, the Directive can also apply to interest payments made to entities behind which individuals could attempt to "hide", called "residual entities". Paying agents must also operate a savings tax regime in respect of payments made to residual entities. Residual entities themselves also have paying agent obligations.

The application of the Directive in respect of payments from hedge funds is ambiguous for a number of reasons. First, the simple terms of the Directive are not easily applied to typical hedge fund structures – investment arrangements can make it difficult to determine whether payments constitute interest or not; in addition, the use of partnerships can give rise to complex residual entity issues. Second, individual country interpretations of the Directive and varying levels of regulation mean that a payment which clearly falls outside scope in one jurisdiction may fall into scope in another.

Furthermore, only certain payments from hedge funds qualify as interest and may be covered under the Directive. Interest is defined broadly and includes items such as payments on distribution from certain collective investment schemes including

Undertakings For Collective Investment in Transferable Securities ("UCITS"), "UCITS equivalent" (see below) funds and collective investment schemes established outside the relevant jurisdictions. As hedge funds rarely make distributions, the impact of this will be limited. However, payments on redemption, sale or refund of shares or units in UCITS, UCITS equivalent funds and collective investment schemes established outside the relevant jurisdictions are also interest if more than 40% of the fund's underlying assets are debt claims (the "40% threshold test").

The UCITS Directive, adopted in 1985, was created to allow open-ended EU funds investing in transferable securities to have a single regulatory regime across the EU. Payments by funds which are established in the EU and which are not UCITS will therefore not be interest under the Directive and so are not within its scope.

Only funds established in EU member states may be UCITS. "UCITS equivalent" funds are funds in the EU dependent territories and third countries which are considered as regulated in an equivalent manner to UCITS funds. In some territories, such as Cayman and British Virgin Islands, only those funds established as retail or licensed funds are considered as UCITS equivalent, hence other funds established in these territories are out of scope. Existing funds in the EU dependent territories and third countries will need to determine whether they are UCITS equivalent funds under the applicable local regulations for their jurisdiction. New funds have the benefit of performing a legal analysis of the fund and the local regulations prior to set-up and can take the results into their structuring plans accordingly as required. However, even if a fund itself is within the scope of a savings tax regime because of its legal status, the payments it makes may still fall out of scope if 40% or less of its underlying assets are debt claims as discussed above.

Despite the label, a hedge "fund" may not be legally constituted as a collective investment scheme. In this case, instead of looking to the rules discussed above, the fund should look to the nature of the financial instrument under which the payment arises (the nature of any underlying assets will usually not be a relevant factor here). Whether the payment is interest or not will depend on the legal definition of interest and local savings tax regulations in the location where the paying agent is established. For example, many feeder funds are established as partnerships. Again, depending on the local rules and regulations, distributions from partnerships may not constitute interest income for the purposes of the savings tax regime. Partnerships can, however, give rise to residual entity issues and payments to them may also be within scope. Therefore, where a hedge fund uses a master fund with partnerships as feeder funds, there are two stages in the payment chain where savings tax issues could arise; from the master to the feeder and from the feeder to individual investors.

APPLICATION OF IFRS TO INVESTMENT FUNDS
Introduction
The financial reporting environment for investment funds is governed principally by the International Accounting Standards Board's ("IASB") two financial instrument standards IAS 32 and 39. These two standards were recently revised for accounting periods commencing in 2005, and will be supplemented by the new standard IFRS 7, which will be effective from 2007 (or sooner if adopted early). IFRS 7, which will become the new disclosure standard for financial instruments, consolidates existing disclosure requirements and introduces some significant new ones, principally the requirement to present a sensitivity analysis. The principal areas of impact of IAS 32 and 39, as they affect investment funds are detailed below followed by an analysis of the impact of IFRS 7. Preparers of financial statements need to be aware of the later implementation date for IFRS 7.

In addition to these three significant standards on financial instruments, there are a number of key differences between IFRS and UK GAAP in the following areas:

❑ cash flow statements (IAS 7);
❑ statement of changes in shareholders equity (IAS 1); and
❑ consolidation of subsidiaries (IAS 27).

Figures in parentheses denote the International Standard.

Convergence of world standards
The analysis below focuses on International Financial Reporting Standards ("IFRS") issued by the IASB. However in the UK and Ireland, there have already been moves towards a convergence of local standards with IFRS. As part of the convergence process the

Accounting Standards Board ("ASB") has issued FRS 25 and FRS 26, based on the revised IAS 32 and 39 respectively. The first application date of the two new FRSs depends on whether the fund is a listed entity or unlisted company. Unlisted entities that are not companies (eg, unlisted unit trusts) will not come within the scope of the new FRSs, a significant difference from IFRS. FRS 25 and 26 are based on the text of IAS 32 and 39, with any small modifications highlighted. In essence, apart from scope (and timing of implementation) differences, the two new FRSs are identical to IFRS.

IAS 32 and IAS 39
IAS 32 – Financial Instruments
"Presentation and Disclosure" deals with disclosure requirements whereas IAS 39: "Financial Instruments – Recognition and Measurement" deals with issues of measurement (and the determination of "fair value"). The principal areas of impact of IAS 32 can be discussed under three headings:

❏ classification of share capital;
❏ offsetting; and
❏ disclosure requirements.

IAS 39 focuses initially on the classification of financial assets and liabilities, as it is this classification which fundamentally determines the valuation (measurement) base. Two distinct measurement bases exist – amortised cost and fair value, with each base applicable only to certain classifications. The classifications are explained below as are the principles of determining fair value under IFRS. This article then looks at two issues that have important consequences for funds – the treatment of transaction costs and the effective interest rate.

IAS 32 "Financial instruments: presentation and disclosure"
Classification of share capital
The effect of IAS 32 is immediately visible in the presentation of the financial statements of most mutual funds following new guidance on the classification of interests (capital) held by shareholders or unit holders. IAS 32 specifies that a financial instrument that gives the holder the right to put it back to the issuer for cash or another financial asset (a "puttable instrument") is a financial liability. It

gives an example of an open-ended mutual fund that provides its unit holders or members with a right to redeem their interests in the fund at any time for cash equal to their proportionate share of the asset value of the fund. In such cases the interest of the shareholders or unit holders must be classified as a liability.

However the standard states that the classification as a financial liability does not preclude the use of descriptors such as "net asset value attributable to unit holders" and "change in net asset value attributable to unit holders" on the face of the financial statements. Accordingly most mutual fund financial statements for 2005 contain such descriptors at the foot of the balance sheet and statement of changes in net assets respectively and an accounting policy to explain the classification of share capital as a liability.

As a consequence of the classification of shareholders/unit holders' interest as a liability, dividends/distributions paid to shareholders/unit holders must be classified as an expense and included in the income statement. Prior to the revised IAS 32, some funds may have put dividends through the statement of changes in net assets but this will no longer be allowed – they must be shown in the income statement of the fund and taken into account in arriving at the "change in net assets attributable to unit holders from operations".

The IASB is currently considering an amendment to IAS 32 in relation to financial instruments puttable at fair value and it is likely that a reversion to an equity classification may be permitted in future periods. The board has not indicated so far any likely timeframe for implementation of the amendment but an exposure draft is expected shortly.

Offsetting

IAS 32 introduces criteria for when an asset and liability should be offset. If the criteria are met, there is no option available – the fund must offset the asset and liability. The following are the criteria for offset:

❑ the fund currently has a legally enforceable right to set off the recognised amounts; and
❑ the fund intends either to settle on a net basis, or to realise the asset and settle the liability simultaneously.

Both conditions must be met, and if they are then a single net amount is shown in the balance sheet (in place of the asset and liability).

Disclosures

IAS 32 specifies disclosures in relation to interest rate risk and credit risk. It also provides that when financial instruments create a potentially significant exposure to these risks or other financial risks (ie, currency risk, market price risk, or liquidity risk) then certain terms and conditions will warrant disclosure. This latter requirement would generally require quantification of currency exposure where significant. Additional disclosures in relation to derivatives might be required where they create a potentially significant exposure to one of the financial risks, and such disclosure might include notional amounts for interest rate swaps, dates at which options may be exercised and the exercise price of options.

Interest rate risk

In disclosing interest rate risk, a fund must indicate which of its financial assets and financial liabilities are exposed to fair value interest rate risk (fixed rate investments); that are exposed to cash flow interest rate risk (floating interest rates) and that are not directly exposed to interest rate risk (such as equity investments). Many funds provide a table of such amounts, but these disclosures can be given within the narrative text.

For each class of financial assets and liabilities, a fund must disclose information about maturity dates (or contractual repricing dates if earlier) and effective interest rates. This information should be provided for fixed rate financial assets and for fixed rate financial liabilities. Information about maturity dates may be given by disclosing the weighted average period to maturity of fixed rate investments or alternatively by given a breakdown of the amount of fixed rate investments into categories maturing in different time periods (eg, between one and two years, between two and three years etc). Weighted average interest rates can be given for classes of financial instruments.

Credit risk

IAS 32 requires that significant concentrations of credit risk be disclosed. Concentrations of credit risk are disclosed when they are not apparent from other disclosures about the nature of the fund's operations and financial position of the fund and result in significant exposure to loss in the event of a default by the other parties. Geographical area or industry may be used as a basis for identifying concentrations of risk. Credit derivative contracts may also create an exposure to credit risk requiring disclosure.

Fair value
The methods and significant assumptions applied in determining fair value for significant classes must be disclosed. Where fair value is determined using a valuation technique (as opposed to by reference to published price quotations) this must be disclosed.

IAS 39: "Financial instruments – recognition and measurement"
Whereas IAS 32 is concerned with disclosures in the financial statements, IAS 39 is principally concerned with determining the amounts at which financial assets and liabilities are reported in the financial statements (measurement). It categorises financial assets and liabilities into four categories and specifies two fundamentally different measurement bases, amortised cost and fair value, which must be used for certain categories. Once an investment has been classified into a certain category, it must use the measurement base that applies to that category. However as we will see below, a certain element of choice comes into determining classification.

Classification of investments
IAS 39 defines four categories of financial assets and liabilities as follows:

❑ at fair value through profit or loss;
❑ held to maturity investments;
❑ loans and receivables; and
❑ available for sale.

Investments classified within the categories of "at fair value through profit or loss" and "available for sale" are measured at fair value. Held to maturity investments and loans and receivables are measured at amortised cost.

Fair value through profit or loss
The category of "at fair value through profit or loss" has two sub-categories: held for trading and those designated upon initial

recognition as at fair value through profit or loss. Held for trading investments are those:

❑ acquired or incurred principally for the purpose of selling or repurchasing in the near term; or
❑ are part of a portfolio of identified financial instruments that are managed together and for which there is evidence of a recent actual pattern of short-term profit taking; or
❑ are derivatives, as derivatives are always classified as held for trading (unless designated an effective hedging instrument, but hedge accounting under IAS 39 in funds is very rare).

Investments that meet the above criteria must be classified as held for trading. For example, equity securities that are bought and sold by a fund (actively traded) should be classified as held for trading.

A financial asset or liability may upon initial recognition be designated at fair value through profit or loss provided that it is part of a group of financial assets, financial liabilities or both that is managed and has its performance evaluated on a fair value basis, in accordance with a documented risk management or investment strategy. Thus almost all investments made by a mutual fund would satisfy this condition and could be designated as at fair value through profit or loss. In practice the two sub-categories of "fair value through profit or loss" will be the most likely classification for a fund's investments.

There is only one type of investment for which measurement at fair value is not an option: equity instruments that do not have a quoted market price in an active market and whose fair value cannot be reliably measured. Such instruments must be measured at cost. IAS 32 includes specific additional disclosure requirements for such instruments.

IAS 32 requires that the carrying amounts of each of the two sub-categories of "fair value through profit or loss" be disclosed separately in the financial statements.

Held to maturity investments

Held to maturity investments are non-derivative financial assets with fixed or determinable payments and fixed maturity that an entity has the positive intention and ability to hold to maturity or than those an entity designates upon initial recognition as at fair value through profit or loss or available for sale; and that do not meet the definition of loans and receivables.

The intention and ability to hold to maturity are key to the classification. It is likely that, for an open-ended investment fund where investors can request redemption of their units and which would require sales of investments to meet such requests, this condition will not be met. Theoretically where it is possible to split a fund's portfolio into a portfolio of held to maturity investments and a distinct portfolio of investments at fair value through profit or loss and this latter portfolio can be shown to be sufficient to meet most reasonably foreseeable redemption requests then classification as held to maturity might be possible.

Loans and receivables

Loans and receivables are non-derivative financial assets with fixed or determinable payments that are not quoted in an active market and that are not classified as held for trading, or designated as at fair value through profit or loss or available for sale. Debt securities that are not quoted in an active market would fall under this classification. For example certificates of deposit and commercial paper would most likely be classified as loans and receivables and measured at amortised cost.

Available-for-sale

The final category includes any investment that does not fall into the other three categories. Available for sale investments are distinguished from those at fair value through profit or loss by the fact that changes in fair value do not go through the income statement but instead are put through the statement of changes in equity. This was a change introduced in the most recent revision of IAS 39. Prior to 2005 entities had a choice of putting fair value changes on available for sale securities through the income statement or through the statement of changes in equity. Such a choice is no longer available. Because of this change, most funds will no longer choose to use this classification as most funds wish to show all fair value changes in the income statement. The principle benefit of using an available for sale classification arises from the treatment of transaction costs, which is explained below.

Measurement of fair value

Two of the above classifications – "fair value through profit or loss" and "available for sale" – require constituent assets and liabilities to be measured at fair value at the balance sheet date. The application guidance to IAS 39 is an integral part of the standard and provides guidance on the measurement of fair value in paragraphs AG69 to AG82. Two fundamentally different market scenarios, requiring differing approaches to the measurement of fair value, are identified in the application guidance – the first where there is an active market and the second where there is no active market.

Active market

An active market exists where quoted prices are readily and regularly available from an exchange, dealer, broker, industry group, pricing service or regulatory agency, and those prices represent actual and regularly occurring market transactions on an arm's length basis. In such cases, the existence of published price quotations is the best evidence of fair value and when they exist they are used to measure the financial asset or financial liability. IFRS requires the use of bid/ask pricing as explained below in this case.

No active market

If the market for a financial instrument is not active, fair value should be measured using a valuation technique. Such techniques include reference to recent arm's length market transactions, reference to the current fair value of a similar instrument, discounted cash flow analysis and option pricing models. If there is a valuation technique commonly used by market participants and that technique has been shown to provide reliable estimates of prices obtained in actual transactions, then that technique should be used. The valuation technique should be tested periodically by reference to observable market transactions.

Bid/ask pricing

Under IAS 39, in an active market the appropriate quoted price for an asset held is usually the current bid price and for a liability held is the asking price. This method of valuation will for many funds be different from the method specified in the fund's offering documents. Funds which are valued using closing trade prices or mid-market prices will accordingly be required to perform a valuation for reporting purposes at the year end using Bid and Ask prices. This bid/ask valuation should be used as the value of assets and liabilities in the financial statements and reconciliation may then be provided to another valuation basis eg, mid/closing/last traded as per the offering memorandum or prospectus.

When a fund has assets and liabilities with offsetting market risks (eg, long and short positions in the same security), it may use mid-market prices for establishing fair value for the offsetting positions and apply the bid or ask price to the net open position as appropriate. When current bid and asking prices are unavailable the price of the most recent transaction provides evidence of the current fair value as long as there has not been a significant change in economic circumstances since the time of the transaction.

Transaction costs

Transaction costs are defined as incremental costs that are directly attributable to the acquisition, issue or disposal of a financial asset or liability. They include fees and commissions paid to agents, advisers, brokers and dealers as well as levies, transfer taxes and duties.

For financial instruments classified as at fair value through profit or loss, transaction costs are immediately recognised in profit or loss on initial recognition. For many funds such costs had been included in the cost of the investment but they are now required to be expensed as incurred. Transaction costs that would arise on disposal should not be deducted from quoted prices in arriving at fair value at the balance sheet date.

For financial instruments that are carried at amortised cost, transaction costs on purchase are included in the initial cost. Transaction costs on available for sale securities can also continue to be included within the cost of the investment.

Effective interest rate

Held to maturity investments and loans and receivables are carried at amortised cost in the financial statements. Amortised cost is required to be calculated using the effective interest rate method. This method allocates interest income/expense to accounting periods by applying the effective interest rate to the carrying amount of the asset/liability.

Interest on available for sale securities is also required to be calculated using the effective interest rate method. The method must even be used to calculate interest on debt securities that are carried at fair value, as IAS 18 "Revenue" requires that all reported interest income be calculated using the effective interest rate. However the requirement under IAS 18 is not currently mirrored under Irish and UK GAAP.

The effective interest rate is the rate that exactly discounts estimated future cash payments or receipts through the effective life of the financial instrument (or shorter period if appropriate) to the net carrying amount of the financial asset or financial liability.

The effective interest rate needs to be calculated for floating rate investments and not just for fixed interest rate investments. For floating rate investments, an effective interest rate will be calculated at the outset based on the cash flows foreseen at that date. When subsequently cash flows are re-estimated to reflect movements in market rates of interest the effective interest rate is recalculated at that time.

IFRS 7 "Financial instruments: disclosures"

IFRS 7 will take effect for accounting periods commencing on 1st January, 2007 or later. Earlier adoption is possible. Where a fund waits until 2007 to implement IFRS 7 it will be required to show comparative figures in compliance with the standard. FRS 29 the UK standard that implements this IFRS takes effect at the same time as the international standard.

IFRS 7 requires that the net gains or net losses on each of the four classes of financial assets and liabilities be disclosed separately in the financial statements. Separate disclosure will be required of net gains or losses on financial assets and liabilities held for trading and of net gains or losses on financial assets or liabilities designated as at fair value through profit or loss upon initial recognition. Some reorganisation of fund accounting systems to provide this information may be necessary.

This new standard also introduces a new disclosure requirement in relation to market risk. The standard requires that a sensitivity analysis be presented for each type of market risk to which the entity is exposed at the reporting date. Market risk comprises interest rate risk, currency risk and other price risk (eg, equity price risk or commodity price risk). The sensitivity analysis should show how profit or loss and equity would have been affected by changes in the relevant risk variable that were reasonably possible at the balance sheet date.

An analysis of financial liabilities indicating the remaining contractual maturities of the financial liabilities is also required in order to illustrate liquidity risk. This will generally be presented by dividing liabilities into time bands by maturity date. IAS 32 contained no such specific disclosure requirement although it required certain terms of financial instruments (including maturity dates) to be disclosed where they gave rise to a significant exposure to liquidity risk.

IFRS versus *UK GAAP – key differences in other standards*

Application of IFRS to investment funds
IFRS versus *UK GAAP-key differences in other standards*
Convergence of UK GAAP and IFRS, particularly in relation to financial instrument standards, has meant that there are not that many significant differences between the different GAAP any more. Many of the differences that a reader of the financial statements might notice arise from disclosure requirements of regulatory bodies and legislation. The convergence process essentially involves adopting UK standards based on IFRS with no changes other than those that are essential or justifiable. The process is ongoing with the ultimate aim to eliminate all differences between UK GAAP and IFRS over the next three to four years. There are currently still a few key differences, the most significant of which are explained below.

Cash flow statements
Under IFRS, preparation of a cash flow statement is mandatory-no exemption is available. All funds preparing financial statements in accordance with IFRS must include a cash flow statement. This contrasts with UK GAAP where an exemption is available to open-ended investment companies from preparing a cash flow statement if certain conditions are met. The conditions for exemption are:

❑ Substantially all of the entity's investments are highly liquid
❑ Substantially all of the entity's investments are carried at market value; and
❑ The entity provides a statement of changes in net assets.

In practice almost all open-ended investment funds will meet these conditions and it is rare to see a cash flow statement presented under UK GAAP. Closed ended funds cannot avail of this exemption.

IAS 7 Cash flow statements deals with how a cash flow statement should be prepared under IFRS. Cash flows should be grouped under three headings: operating activities, investing activities and financing activities. The statement should show the movement in cash and cash equivalents, which include certain short-term highly liquid investments.

EFAMA, the European Fund and Asset Management Association, is currently making representations to the IASB to request that an exemption from preparing a cash flow statement be introduced into IAS 7, similar to that available in UK GAAP and US GAAP.

Statement of changes in shareholders equity

Under IAS 1, a statement of change in shareholders equity must be presented as part of the financial statements. IAS 1 requires that, as part of this statement or in the notes to the financial statements, a reconciliation should be given between the carrying amount of each class of contributed equity and each reserve at the beginning and end of the period, separately disclosing each change. For a fund with for example 15 sub-funds and each containing say 4 share classes, this requirement becomes quite onerous. The statement of changes in shareholders equity is equivalent to the statement of changes in net assets required under US GAAP. Under UK GAAP, the authorised fund SORP requires the preparation of a statement of changes in shareholders' net assets, however analysis by share class in this statement is not required.

Consolidation of subsidiaries

Past practice for master–feeder fund structures, where the feeder owned more than 50% of the participating share capital of the master fund, has been not to consolidate the master fund in the feeder financial statements. This is currently the practice under UK GAAP and US GAAP. However IAS 27 (revised) requires the issue of consolidation to be reconsidered and may require that certain master–feeder structures be consolidated. Particular attention needs to be given to situations where the master fund may be considered to be a SPE under SIC-12. At present however consolidation is still very rare under IFRS, and EFAMA is seeking to obtain exemptions similar to those available in the US.

CONCLUSION

The effect of FRS 25/26 and IAS 32/39 (as revised) is now evident in many financial statements. There are still some entities (unlisted companies under UK and Irish GAAP) which will only changeover to the new requirements for 2006 year ends. Shortly thereafter changes in disclosures will be required by IFRS 7/FRS 29 if not adopted earlier.

The IASB is continuing to work to revise and update IAS 32 and 39 where it considers there is a need for a revision or update, and currently has a number of projects under way. Most of these should not result in any significant changes for funds. One area where change has been suggested by many parties is the classification of shareholders/unit holders interests as a liability under IAS 32, and the IASB is expected to release in 2006 an exposure draft on the issue of financial instruments puttable at fair value.

---

1 § 882(b).
2 See generally *Spermacet Whaling & Shipping Co. v. Commissioner*, 30 TC 618 (1958), aff'd, 281 F2d 646 (6th Cir. 1960).
3 See *Liang v. Commissioner*, 23 TC 1040, 1043 (TC 1955).
4 See Prop. Regs. § 1.864(b)–1(a).
5 § 864(b)(2)(A), 864(b)(2)(B).
6 See Id.
7 See generally § 897.
8 § 954(c), § 1297(b)(1).
9 Treas. Reg. § 1.1295–1(g).
10 § 1296(a)(1).
11 26 USC § 951(a)(1).
12 26 USC § 951(b).
13 26 USC § 954(a).
14 See § 513(a).
15 IRC § 149(a)(3)(A).
16 IRC § 163(f)(2)(B); IRC § 871(h)(2)(A).

17 26 CFR 1.1441–2(b)(3).

18 IRC § 871(g)(1).

19 IRC § 861(c).

20 IRC § 871(i)(2)(B) and 881(d).

21 Under the Directive interest is defined fairly broadly and includes interest paid or credited relating to debt claims and also payments on distribution and redemption from certain collective investment schemes.

22 A paying agent is an entity which makes or secures a payment of interest to an individual.

Index